Life Messages for Moms

INSPIRATION FOR A MOTHER'S SPIRIT

JOSEPHINE CARLTON

MJF BOOKS
NEW YORK

Published by MJF Books
Fine Communications
322 Eighth Avenue
New York, NY 10001

Life Messages for Moms
LC Control Number 2004115222
ISBN 13: 978-1-56731-643-8
ISBN 10: 1-56731-643-3

This book is dedicated to my three magnificent children,

Lisa, Abbie, and Michael, who inspire me and

are a testimony of my deepest love, and to my angelic

mother, in remembrance of her unselfishness, brilliance,

kindness, and unconditional love.

Contents

Introduction

❦

This volume collects heartfelt testimonials on mother-hood by twenty-seven remarkable women from all walks of life. In a series of interviews, I elicited their reflections on twelve different aspects of motherhood, which form the chapters of this book.

The process of connecting to the women I interviewed became a marvelous journey for me. Their messages were profound and inspiring, and collectively constitute a tribute to mothers everywhere. Is there any work more important than being a mother? What could be more important than creating life itself? What has more impact on the world than nurturing children on their journey to adulthood? Who besides our mothers has a greater influence on the people we become? Motherhood is a complex experience filled with challenges and pain as well as joy and growth. As you will see, the radiant joy of being a mother shines through the thoughts of the women you will meet in this book.

This work was a natural extension of my first book, *Life Messages: Inspiration for the Woman's Spirit*, which was dedicated to my mother's memory. My own children have always told me that I should write a book about the experience of being a mother, and I believe that to thrive as a mother, one must be responsive to one's own children. So, I've taken them up on the challenge, and the result is this book.

I am blessed to be the child of a woman who was, in all

respects, an incredible mother. My only regret is that she died unexpectedly at the age of fifty-nine when my first child was only a year old, and that she was not with me for the births of my next two children. She would have enjoyed being a loving grandmother to all of my children. I know in my heart that she lives within them, because I *see* it every time I look into their eyes. Her gentle spirit of love and goodwill dwells within them. My mother's legacy of love is her gift to all of us. She exemplifies the message of this book's concluding chapter: Motherhood Lasts Forever.

I want to thank all the women who shared their wisdom and selflessness with me for this project. Bless all of you. May your messages of love inspire mothers everywhere.

JOSEPHINE CARLTON
Marin County, California
www.josephinecarlton.com

Life Messages
for Moms

Chapter 1

The Meaning of Motherhood

*Motherhood is the ultimate reward and the
ultimate sacrifice, all in the same breath.*

LAUREL BIEVER

"What does motherhood mean to you?" This deceptively simple question provoked a multitude of eloquent reflections from the mothers I interviewed. To many of them, the miracle of giving birth was an experience beyond explanation, one that led to changes and discoveries they never could have foreseen. Despite the variety of meanings that emerged, the shared experience of giving and nurturing life creates a common ground among all mothers.

The creation of life is a divine gift, and commands the utmost reverence. It is also the beginning of a journey to self-discovery. Mothers achieve a new understanding of love and unselfishness that radiates through the rest of their lives. Yet the reflections of these women disclose not only the miraculous joy of becoming a mother, but also the idea that motherhood is both "the ultimate reward and the ultimate sacrifice."

The variety of responses intrigued me. For some, *giving* is the essence of motherhood while others believe motherhood itself is the gift. Some speak of motherhood's rewards, both large and small, while others ponder leaving a legacy that will carry on through many generations. But every woman I interviewed presented me with an inspiring story hinging on her own unique meaning of motherhood.

Carmel Greenwood

Author/Entrepreneur/Lecturer

– Mother of 5 –

Motherhood means a loving, a sharing, a nurturing of a child and nurturing of the child's spirit. I see so many parents squash this spirit, and that is the most crucial thing that you can give to a child—to love and nurture them for who they are, not for who you want them to be. To bring out their innate qualities and gifts and to let them shine and let them be who they are.

Motherhood requires a lot of standing back. You allow them to make their own mistakes. You can't make it all okay for them because the more you do that, the more they will make bigger and bigger messes for you to clean up.

I felt like the garbage lady at one stage, marching in and cleaning up all these big messes. Ultimately we are responsible for our messes, and our biggest gift is helping our children grow up to be independent and responsible people. So as mothers if we keep taking away their lessons, they have to keep repeating and repeating and repeating until you allow them to get it. I've been the biggest one not doing that with my eldest daughter because I would make it all okay for her. It took years for us to play this game and repeat the same thing over and over again till we both got it.

The degree to which you hate someone is the degree to which you love somebody. I got to the stage where I was ready to really strangle this girl because that was the degree that I wanted her to be straight and off drugs. So I would not say a mother's role is easy. It was much easier running a financial institution than being a mother. It's the most difficult role on the planet.

Isabel Allende

Author

– Mother of 2 –

Motherhood for me is extended to many people, not only my children. It's something that really reaches out for many people. I lost my daughter years ago, and I have tried to replace her many times with different young women that I tried to protect, that I keep very close to me in my life and in my heart. I have a son that I adore and my grandchildren that I always call my children. I forget that they are my grandchildren, and I really interfere in their lives terribly. I also am a mother for my daughter's husband, who is now remarried, and his wife. I'm a big matriarch. I think that's my vocation.

Virginia Harris

Spiritual Leader

– Mother of 3 –

I don't think of motherhood so much as an event but more as a way of living each day, each moment. I really try to live my motherhood as the expression of God's mothering of the world. I try to mother everyone in every situation. I try to bring the motherhood qualities to the boardroom or walking on the beach. I think it's really important that those mothering qualities go out beyond the door and not just cling to the hearth.

We are mothered by so many others wherever we are. Basically, I think, women probably allow themselves to be mothered more than men. Carried too far, that can lead to abuse, but I think that needs to be something that we accommodate in society as very, very acceptable, for both men and women to be mothered and to mother. I love it when men express more of their motherhood without any reservation or even stopping to think if this is okay, to hug someone or to load or unload the dishwasher, or some of those stereotypical things, to be the emotional caregiver as well as the physical and financial provider. To me, that is a real joy, to see men expressing that.

Jennifer Morla

Entrepreneur/Designer

– Mother of 2 –

Motherhood means giving and getting twice as much back. That is motherhood to me. My two girls, Petra and Zara, who are seven and eight, are my therapy. I have a career in design and have had my office for twenty years. I work about six hours a day at my studio. I am here to get the kids off in the morning, and I am there at six o'clock at night. My husband drives them to school. What we have is nearly ideal. I e-mail teachers in the morning and get a handle on what is happening with their homework and social life. I try not to do errands on the weekends. I take them ice skating and do other activities with them. Making them feel safe and secure is important to me. You stay younger by having children to a certain degree because they keep you current with whatever is happening. I don't know what I would do without my children. We have a joyous and warm family connection when we are together. I come home and the moment I cross the threshold, it is immediate attention to them. I do not think about work while they're around.

Although it takes a lot of giving, motherhood is unqualified love. It's allowing those children to be the center of the universe. In a way, they're always your center of the universe, to a certain degree. I had my family late in life. Even though it wasn't by design, I felt "When I'm forty, I'm going to have kids." It's worked out very well for me, because I'm also at a point where there's a maturity that I can give to my children. I believe part of what motherhood is about is that you are providing a diversity of experiences, either intuitively or by design, to your children. Being a woman, a mother, a career woman, and a teacher, it's amazing how all of these duties overlap. These roles are not as discrete as we might think.

As mothers, we are nurturing in many different ways. Say you have an office of employees; you're being a mom or a babysitter half the time anyway. You want to provide a nurturing environment where you're not directing somebody, but allowing his or her ideas to flourish, and that's what you're trying to do as a mother.

Judith Epstein

Appellate Judge

– Mother of 2 –

Presently, I'm an appellate judge for the State Bar Court, which is the administrative court for the Supreme Court. For twenty-five years, I was a practicing attorney, both as a partner in a law firm, and then, as general counsel for a multinational company. Prior to that, I clerked at our State Supreme Court and, before that, I went to law school.

Throughout that entire time I was also a mother. I met my husband at age seventeen. We dated, got married at the age of twenty-one, and had my first child at the age of twenty-three, my second one at the age of twenty-four.

In a sense, I would say that motherhood is the emotional center of my universe. In contrast, I'd say that my career is the intellectual center of my universe. So what you really have are two universes, if you will, and sometimes they exist synergistically, and sometimes they exist antagonistically. But both of those universes define to me who I am. I guess the third universe would be my relationship with my life partner, my husband. Sometimes these universes overlap; sometimes they operate independently. But I would say motherhood is the superior and most abiding center of my universe.

Laurel Biever

Counselor/Therapist

– Mother of 1 –

I have a daughter, soon to be four, who is now the light of my life. She's beautiful, smart, fun to be with. I can't say enough things about her.

I am a widowed mother. I like to make that differentiation between single mother and widowed mother because it seems very different to me. My husband passed away the day after Julia was born, and so Julia and I have been going through this journey together with plenty of support and wonderful family and friends in my life as well.

Motherhood is an ever-changing thing. What I thought it was going to be in the beginning is much different than it is and, I'm sure, than what it will be. But when it comes down to it, motherhood is the ultimate reward and the ultimate sacrifice, all in the same breath. It really puts life into perspective having someone be dependent on you and look to you for love and guidance. What it does for me is bring out the purest kind of love I have ever experienced.

Yasmine Ahmed McGrane

Entrepreneur

– Future mother –

I was born and raised in Montreal. My father was originally from Pakistan. He grew up with a lot of hardship and immigrated to London, where he met my mother. After maybe about six or eight months they ended up getting married. They didn't know the same language, but they had three children, and I'm the youngest of the three. I think what my parents gave to me was a wonderful lesson about embracing diversity and what it takes to become a mother and the intuitive part of being a mother and living your life from your heart.

My mother is really my soul-inspirer in my life. Through my thirty-five years she's been a place in my heart where there's always a source of inspiration. When I look at my mother and feel my mother, it's always a feeling of creativity. She was just a source of creativity in everything she did.

Today it's a rainy day here, and I'm one of those rare birds that just loves a good rainy day. And I think a lot of that has to do with who my mother is. Growing up, I remember riding the school bus home from school and if it was pouring rain outside, I would just get this really wonderful fuzzy feeling inside because I knew that on rainy days our dining table was cleared out and we would just create. My mother was at the table with us, creating Christmas cards from scratch, drawings from scratch. A child can bring out a lot of creativity in your passions. Your own inspirations can finally come out when you are a mother.

Alexia Nye Jackson

Comedienne/Stay-at-Home Mom

– Mother of 3 –

I am the passionate mother of three. I'm forty-three. My children are eleven, eight, and four, so with my husband I'm right in the throes of parenting.

In addition to having made the choice to be a full-time mother, I found myself wanting to make sure that other people have a clear understanding of exactly what it is that we do. It's an old story, but it's true—that motherhood doesn't seem to garner the respect that it deserves. Some people say that's because it's an unpaid or unaccounted labor. But, anyway, in addition to mothering I'd like to think of myself as the messenger of motherhood, only because I do stand-up comedy around that podium.

Someone once said motherhood is like seeing your heart walk around outside of your body. Motherhood is being given the opportunity to revisit the human condition through all of its stages and to know that you have an opportunity to bring people into this world who are aware of others around them and who are loving, giving human beings and everything else that you might want to put in. So motherhood means to me the opportunity to give all the important things in the world and see them come right back to you, because that is really what happens.

Calle Anderson

Artist/Sculptor

– Mother of 2 –

I have brothers who are the same ages as my son. I had my son when I was eighteen, and I had a three-year-old and a one-year-old brother at that time. So the whole issue of having a mother and being a mother and having my family integrated into my mother's family was very unusual and—in the end—a very happy circumstance.

I had my daughter four years later, so I offer the experience of somebody who had children when they were very young. During that time I made up for my education by going to college and graduating. I would say my son was about seven or eight when I graduated from college, and then later I went on to do my graduate work.

I'm a working artist. I show my work in California and in Europe. I was divorced after being married for almost fifteen years and remarried several years later to a man who has had three children. So I've had some experience with step-parenting. Motherhood is so integrated into my very being that it's almost hard to separate from, but it's certainly what makes me feel whole and what makes me feel happy. It's just so much a part of the core of my identity having had my children when I was so young, and having that be an extremely happy experience. I have friends who had children when they were very young and resented it and were angry about the lack of independence, but I never really went through that. I've always been happy to be a mother.

One thing about motherhood—I did find a certain sense of sadness as each stage ended—the infant that began to crawl, the child that began to walk away from you, the first day of school. All those endings had a bittersweet quality for me because I had enjoyed the stage so much.

Elizabeth Colton

Philanthropist/Women's Advocate

– Mother of 2 –

I have a daughter who's almost seventeen and a son who's twenty. This is the first year that they've both been away at school. So I'm a newly experienced "empty nester." I spend almost one hundred percent of my time as a volunteer working to establish the International Museum of Women, which will be opening in San Francisco in 2008.

Giving birth and realizing that the new life has come from you and the father is incredibly inspiring, but it's also incredibly challenging to think that this little baby is to be raised by you and what he or she becomes has a lot to do with what their life is like growing up. We have the responsibility of nurturing and shaping this child to some degree, and yet we all know as mothers you can only do so much because the child certainly has his or her own role to play in that. You play a role in being responsible for keeping them safe, for being this wealth of love that they need, and trying to teach them the values that you hold dear, so that going forward in life they will have the framework on which to base their own decisions. And then the ultimate paradox is that the more successful you are at this, the more independent they become, the sooner they'll leave you and not need you as much.

Gretchen DeWitt

Public Relations

– Mother of 2 –

What does motherhood mean to me? For me it was a gift, it was a blessing, it was what I wanted the most out of my life. There, that's short and sweet.

Tricia LaVoice

Psychologist/Stay-at-Home Mom

– Mother of 4 –

I am mothering six but have given birth to four. We have two teenagers living with us right now who are just trying to get themselves on a good track. We're helping them out. I have in my life taken on a role with my friends where I will step in and help, that is just who I am. Mothering is the essence of what I do. It's so hard to separate myself from mothering because I believe that when you become a mother you *are* a mother. I am as much a mother as I am a woman; I'm as much a mother as I am Irish, Caucasian. It is now just part of me, so I don't look at mothering as something I do. I know that may be different for other mothers, but maybe because I have so many children under my wing right now, that's how I relate to it.

For me it was the only thing to do, and I didn't just need to give life. I needed to give life to four children. We had three children, and my husband said, great, enough. I started working on a Ph.D. I could not get past wanting another child. I would go into the children's room and kiss them goodnight and stand still, and somebody was missing. I was not complete. I was not done. I fought and fought with my husband and actually put my marriage on the line until he understood that having this fourth child wasn't something I wanted to do, it was something I had to do. It was just beyond anything else.

It took about two years for me to get my husband to understand where I was coming from. During that time I shared my story with anybody who would sit next to me. I found that there were so many women who shared this need for another child. A very, very few went ahead and had that child they were missing. Other women in their sixties would tell me that they still had regret, and that the void never went away. I have always said that I can lay in my deathbed and I can be sad that I didn't finish my Ph.D., I can be sad that I didn't travel the world, but I will never be sad that I didn't give birth to somebody who I was supposed to give birth to.

Jeannie Brown

Entrepreneur

– Mother of 3 –

I have three daughters, one granddaughter who was born very late, and another granddaughter I'm expecting any moment now. My three daughters have been probably the most important thing in my life. I've had so much fun all of these years with all three of them. The reason I've had so much fun is that, when they start walking and they start playing with dolls, when they want to make cookies and they want to make-believe, then I start my life over. Everything that was old to me starts over, and it is now new. Playing dolls, making the cookies, doing all the things—it's like reliving your life again when you have a child.

Stacy Friedman

Rabbi

– Mother of 2 –

*B*eing a mother is the most wonderful thing that's ever happened to me, and it's the most important role my life. I'm a rabbi in a congregation where there are about one thousand units, so let's say three thousand individuals. And in some way I mother all of them and I help take care of them. But the deepest mother love I have is to my own two sons. It's who I am and everything that I do. There's no separating it. In fact, the other day in my capacity as a rabbi I was talking to a family and I called myself mom just like I do to my kids. So in some ways, I'm always a mom regardless of what I'm doing.

Benita Potters

Entrepreneur/Community Volunteer

– Mother of 2 –

I am a member of the Agua Caliente band of Cahuilla Indians. I was educated in southern California, then moved to New York, where I met my husband. I have two daughters, ages twenty-four and twenty-six.

Motherhood is the best job in the world. It's also the most difficult, complicated, and challenging—always new, always different.

My role as a mother has been very satisfying, and it's kind of surprising because the way I was mothered was complicated and fraught with woe. Mother was a classic narcissist and while that can be really a blast to be around because there's so much going on, there is not much room for anybody else. I think a narcissist is ultimately very lonely, because they are never satisfied. I wanted to be much more open. I learned from her what is important, to be open and accepting and not necessarily the center of attention. Mothering my children has really taught me to take care of myself as well. I've been able to be a mother to myself, which was something I needed desperately to do.

Amy Apollo Ahumada

Boutique Manager

– Mother of 2 –

I'm thirty-three, and I have two beautiful little boys. I have a little nine-year-old, River, whose whole name is Kahawaimalulani, which means the flowing river and the heaven's protection. I have a little two-and-a-half-year-old named Koa. His full name is Kekoanolani, which means the warrior for heaven.

I couldn't be more blessed having my kids in my life. It's really natural for me. When I was a child people used to say, "What do you want to be when you grow up?" And I used to say, "A mommy." I just knew that that's what I was supposed to be and that's what I wanted to be, and I was blown away after having my kids, especially my first one—I was twenty-three—that it was just so natural. Everything seemed to go really easily for me. It's how I relate to it. It's everything that I had hoped it would be, everything I dreamed it would be. And it's what I am, it's who I am.

Gretchen de Baubigny

Community Volunteer/Consultant

– Mother of 2 –

I am sixty-six and the mother of two—Helene, age thirty-seven, and Andre, age thirty-nine. I am active in the community. I love to devote my time primarily to education, whether it's in public education or private education, because if you're educated the sky's the limit.

When I was in my twenties, I wasn't interested in motherhood. I was interested in a career. I was interested in the world. I was interested in becoming famous and recognized for my talent. I wanted to be on the stage, and always got the lead roles. Then I met my husband, Andre, as I was traveling around the country. Prior to him, I was engaged to a young doctor who could do nothing but talk about family, which kind of gagged me. I couldn't see myself having children and being in that mother role. Not just yet. Oh, please put that off! When I met my husband and I noticed how loving he was to his nieces, I thought, this is the right man to marry. He was not only a Renaissance man in so many respects, but he's also lovely with children, so this would be a good man.

After we were married for two years and had traveled quite extensively, I thought, something's missing in our lives, and we decided we would start a family. It was fun carrying a child. I was happy that my body was such that I could carry a child and no one would really notice. Then there was the miracle of birth, and I could not believe that exhilarating, incredible moment. I say to every woman, I just cannot believe how incredible the miracle is, and that moment when you feel so closely connected to God that this human being is now on this earth.

I wasn't at all prepared to love the way I love my children. I didn't know that such a boundless love could exist and that I could just give my whole self so recklessly to these beings. Motherhood is a gift from God, and it is a miracle. It is a constant miracle that occurs every single day.

Barbara Rosenberg

Community Volunteer/Philanthropist

– Mother of 2 –

My husband and I have two wonderful sons, Michael and Peter. One is forty-four, and one is forty-two. Each is married to a wonderful woman. We are blessed with five grandsons, Joe, Jake, Jack, Max, and Cyrus.

I don't like to be described by a title—for example, mother. I'm a mother. I'm a mother in-law. I'm a grandmother. I'm a wife. I'm a teacher. I'm a person who holds a doctorate degree, so you can call me Doctor. I think sometimes it's appropriate to assume those roles, but I don't see motherhood as the key to my identity. It's only one aspect of who I am, and that's how I relate to it. I think that my other activities bring to the sense of motherhood more experience and more exposure.

Carol Bartz

Entrepreneur

– Mother of 1 –

To me motherhood is the quintessential thing that we're all about. It's completeness in our lives. It stretches us farther than we could ever imagine. It gives us more joy and sorrow than we could ever imagine. It's a lifelong job. Once you are a mother you always are a mother first and foremost, even as you look around and want to nurture kids around you.

It just changes the way you are. I think it's easier for me to say because I was forty when I had my daughter, so I really was very clearly a non-mother until I was forty. To be honest, I didn't actually look below eye level. I didn't really see kids until I had my daughter, and now I'm checking out kids all the time.

Mary Poland

Philanthropist/Stay-at-Home Mom

– Mother of 1 –

I've been married for twenty-two years. My husband's name is Bill. We worked very hard for a number of years to finally get our son, Stratton, who is thirteen years old now. So it was a very high-energy adventure, or voyage, to get him. We were thrilled when we finally had him, so he's our miracle child.

I've never thought of the word "motherhood" as a meaning per se, but what springs to my mind is the thought of an individual, a human being—that you are able to be a part of their life and you know instinctively that they're going to be in your mind. To me it's a feeling of life always being perpetual in eternity. This may sound morbid, but when I pass away, there will be somebody who will remember me, and I'll continue living on through them.

When I think of my motherhood, I think of my own mom, who was so wonderful with me. I celebrate her every day of my life even though she's passed away now. There are times every day when, being a mother, I could see mom doing the same thing, and so I know that she definitely lives inside of me. I can almost hear my mother's voice saying "I'm so proud of you!" She made a conscious effort to pass positive reinforcement to me, especially compliments from other people. She displayed unabashed sweetness to me. It internally raised the bar for me and my self-esteem. It made me want to please her. I tell Stratton complimentary words from other people about his talent at the piano and his wonderful manners. That's the kind of gift that I'd like to be able to give to my child, and there's nothing that can compare to that.

It's a title that I wear proudly. I was very much molded by the corporate world and learned a lot about being organized and follow-through, and I just had this way of running my life like a business. When my son came into my life, it wasn't a business any longer. It was this feeling of having something much, much more important to do. I guess it's because Bill and I worked so hard to get Stratton that we're very proud of these jobs that we have of being parents.

Arlene Ackerman

School Superintendent

– Mother of 2 –

I'm superintendent of public schools in San Francisco. I'm divorced. I have two sons. Anthony is thirty-one, and Matthew is twenty-eight.

Motherhood to me is the greatest gift that God's ever given me. I have friends who weren't able to have children, and I always felt badly for them because I have always enjoyed my role as a mother. Most people see me as this professional woman who does a lot of things and is successful in her career. But the role that I like most is my role as a mother. I believe it's a gift that allows me to touch and even shape the future. It's a gift that allows me to pass on the legacy of my family history, my mother, my father. They all live on through my children. To me it's the most important role that I have, and every day I'm thankful that I have Anthony and Matthew in my life.

Donna Radu

Equity Trader/Stay-at-Home Mom

– Mother of 2 –

The day I became a mother, at forty years old, I basically arrived. My life has been so enhanced since then. I think life begins with motherhood, and it means everything to me.

Motherhood all by itself has transformed me into a real woman. I have so much more purpose in my life. I believe that everything I say and do will have some kind of an impact or an effect on my children—the words that I use, how I talk to them, the choices I make.

I work very hard at staying in the present all the time with my kids. There are lots of ways to do it. I do a lot of floor time. I always get down on their level, and I'm in the moment. I have to talk to myself about that all the time so I don't lose patience or get frustrated. I try to figure out exactly what's going on, how they're feeling, what time of day it is, and where they're at. When we have issues or problems, or when they act out or have their little temper tantrums, we go to a peace table. We take turns talking. I make sure I have eye contact. I get down on their level. I get down on my knee or whatever. And I look them right in the eye because only when I look them in the eye can I completely appreciate where they are. I don't have to raise my voice because it melts me. Sometimes I cry because I'm so tired. You know, it's a lot of work. It's so much easier to say no.

Anita Figueredo

Physician/Co-Worker of Mother Teresa

– Mother of 9 –

I have nine children and I've lost three so I'm very much aware of what it is to be a mother.

I was the first woman surgeon in San Diego, and for fifteen years I was the only one. And at that time I had five children under five. My mother thought I was out of my mind. She couldn't imagine what was going on in my mind.

I'm an only child, and I thought it was fine. I didn't know what it was like to have brothers or sisters, and I didn't miss them because I was always at boarding school and had plenty of other company. But my husband, Bill, was one of seven, and he seemed to love that and had good relationships with his brothers and sisters. He's a pediatrician. He was the one who loved babies. The babies didn't interest me terribly much. As they got older and had ideas and wanted to express things, then I became fascinated with each child. So I didn't have an innate love for little babies at all. I was perfectly willing to accept them, but it wasn't that phase of their lives that fascinated me. Bill was notorious for always having a child in his arms. He just loved them and was a marvelous pediatrician as a result.

My children are the biggest things in my life. They're devoted to me, and they show me their love and affection. I'm surrounded by them all the time.

Chapter 2

The Gift of Unconditional Love

I disagree that love is just an emotion.
Love is a decision.

ARIEL BYBEE

A mother's love for her child is the strongest love of all; it is an innate, natural love given without reservation. The reflections of the women in this chapter offer a variety of perspectives on the nature and significance of this special brand of love.

What do people mean when they say that a mother's love is "unconditional?" How does it impact a child's well-being? What does it mean for the mother?

Unconditional love is love that is offered without any expectation of reciprocation. Yet these mothers acknowledge that they do have expectations and hopes for their children, and several of them distinguish in their own ways between unconditional love and a permissive parenting style. And, although nothing is more instinctive than a mother's love, learning to love unconditionally is both a choice and a challenge.

The underlying theme in the following messages is the importance of making a child feel loved, and of demonstrating that love as often as possible.

Carmel Greenwood

Author/Entrepreneur/Lecturer

– Mother of 5 –

$\mathcal{M}$otherhood means nurturing, unconditional love, but a toughness as well. I've got five children, and two of my eldest children were addicted to drugs. My daughter's been in jail a couple of times, and every time she's astounded that I show up. And it means never giving up, never turning away. To love your children, no matter what they do, is unconditional love. It means being there—not buying into any nonsense, but being there.

Isabel Allende

Author

– Mother of 2 –

$\mathcal{I}$ think that probably a mother's love is more unconditional than others, but not totally. For example, I see around me women that have several children, and their relationship to a son or daughter depends very much on what they receive back. Of course, you can love your children a lot and for a long time without getting anything back. But there's a point in your life when you relate more to those with whom the relationship is a two-way street in which you give and you receive. Although in my case, with my mother and with my children, it seems unconditional, I think it is because we all give a lot back.

In my family that's the way it has been. With my mother, I have a very close relationship, but she gives me a lot. She has always been there for me in the very present, I think in an almost unconditional way. Of course, she would have loved it if I was more like her, but I wasn't. Eventually, she ended up accepting the person I am.

I communicate with my mother every single day. I call her or I write her a fax or an email every day. And if I don't do it, I feel that something is missing in the day. It has become such a long habit that I just can't break it, and I don't want to.

I have a wonderful relationship with my son. I see him almost every day. I talk to him every day. I'm in every detail of his life, and he is in mine. So it looks like an unconditional love, but that is because we get so much from the other person.

Virginia Harris

Spiritual Leader

– Mother of 3 –

I'm a mother of three sons who are grown. Two are married, and one of them is engaged. I'm a grandmother of five grandsons. I had three brothers growing up, and so I've been raised and lived in a house of men.

I definitely think a mother's love is unconditional. I also think a father has the expression of unconditional love. I love the thought from the Bible, "God is love." I think unconditional love is what I equate with God—universal, impartial, forgiving, encouraging, only seeing the best, the right, in each one of us. I think that we all need to understand that the quality of love and the expression of love all come from the same well, the same source, the same fountain, and that's God. It's like the sun is the source of light, true light, not artificial or manufactured light, but true light.

As the sun shines warmly, and that same brightness and potential brightens everything, so God's love is. That to me is the sense of mother's love that is available and unconditional for everyone.

Unconditional love is love that remains love even if it doesn't meet any response. It's love without an object or an action to call it forth. You love in the face of anger or criticism or betrayal. I don't think it's a doormat that can be abused, but everyone understands that it's not their own love but it's their love from that deeper source, that deeper well in the face of abuse or anger or betrayal or disappointment. That love gives one an inner strength, a spiritual poise, a grace, a calm, a safety.

Ann Getty

Philanthropist/Interior Designer

– Mother of 4 –

I'm a mother and a grandmother, and, of course, I've taken my duties very seriously. It's something one does quite naturally, and it's a large chunk of my life. Between being a mother and a grandmother, mostly I've enjoyed it. I had four boys, so there was a testosterone high, at which point I wanted to escape, but I never had to bail anyone out of jail. That's about the best I can say.

The significance of unconditional love takes a lot of swallowing sometimes, when they can be brutes. But you swallow that and try to keep communicating with them. That's important to me. Loving them, guiding them, no matter how old they are, not interfering all the time. Every once in a while my children want my advice.

Alexia Nye Jackson

Comedienne/Stay-at-Home Mom

– Mother of 3 –

The love of a mother has to be unconditional. It's also a sacrificial job. You put a lot of things aside and realize that this is the priority, and that's just how it has to be. You have another human being in your hands, and this is the priority.

My son Max, for example, was diagnosed with juvenile diabetes when he was seven and a half. It was a big surprise to us and certainly a huge adjustment for Max at that age. So there is something where it's just bigger than those everyday things that are big enough on their own. It's already a huge job to bring a human being into adulthood with all the necessary components of a giving, loving, intelligent individual. To also know that they have a special need physiologically or in any other capacity, you really have to be on your toes and be prepared to give whatever other things they might need.

So many things happen with young children. My greatest fear is that most adults don't have their mental disposition at the age of the child they're with. It's a difficult thing to do, and I work it all the time, but I think that's one of the main things that you should try to do as a parent is to get yourself at their developmental level. I knew that Max was going to have to go through this process of adding something very new to his life and that he would have to be a much more aware person in a lot of ways, being a juvenile diabetic and being insulin dependent. You have to say to yourself he's seven and a half—how does he look at it? It doesn't matter if you're forty-three or you're thirty-eight or whatever your adult age is. You don't really matter.

Somebody said that it's the big things you can handle. It's the day-to-day life that'll kill you. I can go along with that. Little tiny things might mean a ton to some kid.

Elizabeth Colton

Philanthropist/Women's Advocate

– Mother of 2 –

You always love your children no matter where they are or what they're doing. They are always part of you.

Achieving unconditional love is something you have to work at. It's difficult. I don't believe it's a given. To love them, but also to accept them the way they are, takes a lot of practice. To be able to instill in them a certain set of values, and also to be able to support them in who they are, and find out who they are—it's a difficult balance, and it's one that you learn as you go along, starting with love. I think that's what you can always come back to.

Gretchen DeWitt

Public Relations

– Mother of 2 –

I always enjoyed my son. My daughter was more difficult, so there were times that I would not enjoy her company. But I never stopped loving her, and I never loved her less.

The significance is that love never dies, that it's something that I want to count on and that I want the people I love to be able to count on from me.

I consider motherhood to be joyous and fulfilling to the maximum degree. I also consider motherhood sometimes disappointing and challenging and hard work, but anything that's worth having is hard work.

Tricia LaVoice

Psychologist/Stay-at-Home Mom

– Mother of 4 –

I hope I'm not being naive in feeling that every mother's love is unconditional, but I think it's almost instinctual. As an example of this, I was giving birth to my first child, and there were complications, and I closed my eyes. I could hear everything going on in the delivery room, and there was a lot of chaos. I was praying, just save me. If she—the baby—has to go, it's all right, but just save me. And I meant that. Seconds later she was born. And once she was handed to me, I would walk through fire for that child. It was almost as if something turned in me. I had to experience it and actually hold her and see her. As much as I was a mother as she was coming down the birth canal, once I held her it was completely different.

So being unconditional, that's just instinctual. It's like the mother bird that will peck your eyes out if you go near her nest. Without unconditional love for children, how difficult mothering can be. Without the unconditional love, could we have continued as a human race? I don't know.

To love a child not unconditionally is like not feeding them. What could be worse for a child than to be raised in a home where it feels conditional love? I hope I'm not being naive. I hope that every mother shares that with me.

Jeannie Brown

Entrepreneur

– Mother of 3 –

Motherhood periodically is joyous. You go through all kinds of emotional periods in a lifetime. My daughter being fifty-five now, we've had wonderful moments, we've had moments of sadness, we've had moments of tragedy, and we've had moments of decisions, major decisions in our life. You name an emotion, my daughter and I have gone through it. That's what it's all about—pulling together through all of these emotions. If your daughter is sad because her boyfriend doesn't like her, it's a very heavy emotion on the child, and you go through that with her. You live every emotion that your child has.

I think that it's a feeling and the respect that I have earned from my children that makes it an unconditional love. I so wanted to have children, I so loved my children, and they were always my main direction, my main focus.

Stacy Friedman

Rabbi

– Mother of 2 –

I grapple with that word "unconditional," and I don't know exactly what it means. Does it mean I love my children no matter what they do? Of course I love them no matter what they do. But I also see my role as a mother as helping to shape them and guide them and give them direction, let them know the right way to be in the world. I certainly know it's unconditional, but so is the love of a father and so is a love toward my husband and toward other people in my family. If anything, loving my children helps me to love other people in my life better.

Benita Potters
Entrepreneur/Community Volunteer

– Mother of 2 –

Because I didn't have unconditional love in my life growing up, it was not so easy to demonstrate it in my mothering. It was something I had to learn. I really had to investigate what all of that was about. It was easy for me to experience unconditional love when I had this little tiny thing, a bit of perfection. The learning process of how to always have that feeling is like a romance. When you first fall in love, it's all you can think of. It is so easy to not see your love interest's faults and problems and areas where you're not going to get along. Having a baby is the same sort of thing. We have these tiny, adorable perfections, and they're so little and so cute and perfect that it's very easy to unconditionally love them, even in the middle of the night. It gets more difficult when their personalities come out and they start challenging you. So that learning process is really interesting.

Sylvia Boorstein
Author/Buddhist Teacher

– Mother of 4 –

I had a mother who was the most important shaper of my life. My mother's been dead for more than forty years. I think her spirit is alive and well in me.

I think my mother loved me unconditionally. I never thought for a moment that she didn't. I am the only child of very loving, mild-mannered people, and I cannot in my life remember being rebuked. I think that translated into my caretaking of my children. My children are grown and in their forties, and they tease me now about that. I don't meddle in their lives—I try not to.

Because they know I'm a meditation teacher, people sometimes ask me, how is it to have great peace in your mind all the time? And I laugh. These are people who are not local. People here know I'm a regular person. And I say the greatest peace I have in my heart is shadowed by two words. I'm two words away from losing it. Then everybody wants to know what the two words are. And I say, well, the phone has to ring and someone has to say, "Hello, mom," in a certain tone of voice, and it's all gone. Actually I think my children enjoy that. My son likes to say, "You know, Ma, when I'm fifty-five and you're eighty-five, you'll still be worrying about me."

Gretchen de Baubigny

Community Volunteer/Consultant

– Mother of 2 –

*Y*ou can put UNCONDITIONAL LOVE in capital letters. You can put it all over every fiber of my being. I think it's fundamental to have unconditional love for your children and to be sure that as they mature they understand unconditional love and don't ever take it for granted.

I have encountered adults who have not experienced unconditional love and have not had a firm foundation of love. They have an insecurity all their lives. It cannot be filled in any way. No husband can give it to you. No wife can give it to you. No friend can give it to you. No book can give it to you. If it doesn't come from the main source and it is never there, there is a crippled paralysis about that person in living an expansive, productive life. Unconditional love is a foundation for the future.

Barbara Rosenberg

Community Volunteer/Philanthropist

– Mother of 2 –

*T*he love of a mother, in my view, should not be unconditional, because that could forgive a multitude of sins, many of which you might have been the cause of. I think that when a child is born into the world there is a sense of wonder that you've created this being, and you nurture, protect, feed, clothe, love, and raise the child. But you're also doing other things for your spouse, your family, your parents, and your friends, and you fold that child into that broader family of human beings. When the youngster does something that is wrong, even egregious, he or she should be held to task. I don't mean "I won't love you if you don't do this." The child has to know that he or she is secure in the parental relationship, but certain behavior is necessary for a modicum of living. I have to say that it is not unconditional love.

I also believe that you have to earn your child's respect, just as you need to learn to respect your child. It's a learning process between the two of you or three of you or however many are in the family. And then you also have to have some luck.

Carol Bartz

Entrepreneur

– Mother of 1 –

I think *love* is unconditional, *like* is not. What I mean by that is, I think it's perfectly healthy to get angry with your children and even maybe to come right up against that borderline of almost convincing yourself that you don't love them. But what you have at the moment is a real serious case of dislike.

When I read about some horrible things that children do—how they might treat their families or, the ultimate, kill their families—there have to be times in those mothers' lives when they are stretched beyond belief with their feelings. To some extent it's almost too much of a burden to say it's unconditional love. That's almost like saying that we can lead perfectly balanced lives.

Having said all this, I don't think there is a love that matches the love for a child, the intensity of it. I mean the love of your mate is truly a different kind of love. It's intense in its own way, but it is a very different kind of feeling than what you feel for your child.

I have a ripe fifteen-year-old right now who isn't respecting much of anything. That's when you don't like them too much. I mean you really yearn for those days when it was unconditional like.

Mary Poland

Philanthropist/Stay-at-Home Mom

– Mother of 1 –

I was talking with a couple of my friends about the thought that if we had to sacrifice our life for our husbands, we'd maybe think a few minutes about that, and maybe we wouldn't even do it at all. But when it comes to our child, if my life had to pass for his life to go on, I wouldn't even hesitate. It would be done. Done, done, done, done.

That comes back to how I live. I will live through him

and his memory of me. So, absolutely, I would do anything for him. Absolutely. It's unconditional.

Ariel Bybee

Mezzo-Soprano/Voice Teacher

– Mother of 1 –

I think mother love is unconditional, but there are responsibilities with that love. Creating a child, for some people, doesn't automatically mean you love that child. You grow in love for that child because you're responsible for that child, because that little baby is dependent upon you for everything. And in that dependence your love for that child grows because love is a form of sacrifice, and it's a form of support. You support that little one and because you do, you help that little one develop.

I disagree that love is just an emotion. Love is a decision. It's being willing to give yourself to somebody else unconditionally. So you support this little child physically and emotionally and spiritually, and you help it develop and you encourage it. You sacrifice for the child, and all of that is love. And it's definitely unconditional.

Anita Figueredo

Physician/Co-Worker of Mother Teresa

– Mother of 9 –

*T*here was never any way my children could lose my love, and they still can't. I have a very warm relationship with all my children. Some respond very warmly, and others by nature tend to keep a little distant from people, but you try not to force yourself on them.

They're all different. Absolutely all different. That's one of the things you've got to accept. You're dealing with different individuals. If you accept them for themselves and not try to mold them into your image or whatever you had in mind, your relationship is bound to be much better.

Chapter 3

The Joys of Motherhood

*I am so thankful I was able to have the experience
of being a mom. . . . I couldn't imagine having a
life without it.*

SHARON COHN

The messages in this chapter will bring smiles of recognition to any mother or daughter. Asked to recall their happiest moments as mothers—or with their own mothers—some speak of the transformative experience of giving birth as their most memorable moment. Others recount the delights of everyday life with their children: quiet time reading and drawing; sweet, spontaneous exchanges; sharing in their learning and discovery; and, interspersed among these, countless, unpredictable laughs.

In their remembrances of their own mothers, these women highlight the deep and lasting joy found in life's small moments. A recurring theme of these recollections is the simple power of "just being there," attentively and lovingly, for one's children.

Taken together, these messages make the case that we should try to create as much joy as possible while we cope with the responsibilities of motherhood. Creating happy memories that last a lifetime, for ourselves as well as our children, need not be elaborate or difficult. More than anything, we simply need to *be there*.

Carmel Greenwood

Author/Entrepreneur/Lecturer

– Mother of 5 –

Some of my happiest moments were when the babies were born. It was such a miracle and such a gift to be able to see that child, it's just incredible. After that, the happiest times have been laughing and fun and the jokes that we share and the challenges. I have always worked, and I think it's very important to remain an individual because the stresses of motherhood, being the nurturer, caterer, and just taking care of other people, can be overwhelming. My writing keeps my own sense of individuality. I think my children respect me for that. Motherhood can be very joyous, but it also can be very stressful, depending on what your children do. I learned to be very non-judgmental as a mother and that I can't control them.

Isabel Allende

Author

– Mother of 2 –

I think that the happiest moments with my mother have been those moments when we are doing something very creative. For example, we are in the same room and I am writing and she's painting, and I get up and touch up her painting and she interferes in my writing and I say, "No, you said that before. I don't think that works this time."

I remember once she was going to teach a writing class. We prepared the class together with my daughter. It was three generations working together on a project, and it was fantastic. I think the most joyful moments with my daughter, with my grandchildren, with my mother, have been those moments of creating something together.

I do consider motherhood to be joyful most of the time, although there are moments of great pain. I have gone through a lot of pain because I lost my daughter, but I remember the joy more than I remember the pain.

Virginia Harris

Spiritual Leader

– Mother of 3 –

Probably the happiest moments were seeing the children grow and develop, seeing my children become wonderful little boys and then big boys. I've been made very happy when I've seen my sons, now as men or when they were little boys, shining in challenging situations, when I've seen their motherhood that had shown through and brought that victory or brought that calm. I love to see my sons express their motherhood. I think to me as a mother the happiest moments have not just been when they won the football game, or the soccer game, or gotten A's on their papers. I love it when they express their motherhood without any reservation or even stopping to think if it's okay to hug someone, show sensitivity, or load or unload the dishwasher, or some of those stereotypical things. To be there as that emotional caregiver as well as the physical and financial provider. It is a real joy to see them as men expressing that.

Jennifer Morla

Entrepreneur/Designer

– Mother of 2 –

My sister and I were born on the same day, two years

apart. For many years, I thought that everybody shared the same birthday as his or her siblings. One of the wonderful memories is that my mother had this beautiful set of about thirty German puppets from the 1920s. Every year my mother would do a puppet show for our twin birthday party. She built this big puppet theater out of cardboard, and she actually lit it. She put in electricity and had a chandelier in it, the whole thing. The audience of children was just so there, at this puppet show at which she's doing Cinderella or some sort of fairy tale. Merlin the Magician was always the MC. She really hid herself. I remember thinking I didn't even know my mother was doing this, it was these puppets, and Merlin was the magician.

At the end, she always asked any child in the audience if they had a wish, and they could wish whatever they wanted to Merlin. The children would go up to her, and she said later that sometimes it would break her heart because she would hear about abuse or divorce, family strife. She wasn't trying to get that out of them—it was a wish they'd make. It was heartfelt. I don't remember them saying this. To me it was just a magical memory.

Judith Epstein

Appellate Judge

– Mother of 2 –

*T*he most inexplicably joyous moments were at the birth of each of my children. Those, I think, come the closest to the sense of participating in a miracle that you could ever be privileged to be involved in on this earth.

Motherhood not only is irrevocable, but it permeates everything you do. I think that is because it starts with this sense of the miraculous. That's something that you can never, ever forget. It's inexplicable.

Ann Getty

Philanthropist/Interior Designer

– Mother of 4 –

My best experiences with my own boys were when I would go river rafting with them, because that is a time when they can't escape. If you take them to Paris with you, they're off on their own, but when we river rafted, we could do it for a week, more than that on the Colorado, and every evening we'd have to sit around and talk. Of course, there's the joy in their accomplishments, but being with them, with no interference, no distractions, those were my happiest moments.

Laurel Biever

Counselor/Therapist

– Mother of 1 –

I think it comes down to closeness and connection. The happiest moments with my mother were the times when she was just there. There weren't necessarily words, there weren't judgments. There wasn't anything other than just her being there, holding me. I remember being in her lap and having her hold me and stroke my arm, just loving me. I remember her smiling and laughing, being with me when I was in a happy moment, or just being with me when I was in a sad moment.

As for my daughter, the happiest and most connected moments I felt with Julia were when I breast-fed her. There was such a closeness and such a bond during those

moments. I've never experienced such a beautiful together-
ness as I did with that. Then playing with her, getting down
on the ground and tumbling around and doing those
things—just being with her without any idea of what needs
to be done next, being in the moment with her. That's the
same as with my mother when we were in the moment
together, without any other concerns or considerations.
Those were the most beautiful times.

Alexia Nye Jackson

Comedienne/Stay-at-Home Mom

– Mother of 3 –

I consider motherhood to be a blast. I just think it is a
gas. As a comic and I guess a sensitive person, there's an
awful lot of fodder there if you pay attention. You just have
to pay attention. You should paying attention in life anyway,
but it is one of the top priorities in your life as a parent to
pay attention to your children.

I guess some of the most memorable times with my kids
are lying with them in bed at night. My husband and I go
from room to room, bed to bed, and sometimes it's funny
lying down and sometimes it's poignant, but it's always full of
a lot of love. This is really a very important thing, to make
sure your kids know that they are really loved, so they have
a place to go, they always have a home in their head to go to.

I think that that's probably true of my own mom as well.
We moved fifteen or sixteen or seventeen times by the time
I left college, but home was always with you. If you were a
loved person, wherever you were, you were home, because
you knew who you were. That's really the ultimate thing you
end up giving your children.

I guess the happiest times with my mom, too, were just having her talking with us at night. Being together, pajama-clad, talking about life and about the day and just being goofy together. Being together. I feel the same way about my kids. I'm elated to get up to them every morning.

Calle Anderson

Artist/Sculptor

– Mother of 2 –

The happiest moments I have shared with my mother were when she laughed. I think it's because she was such a disciplinarian. From the time I was a very young child I could remember hearing her laugh in the other room. She used to watch Sid Caesar with my father at night, and the tinkling sound of her complete abandonment to that kind of joy was really wonderful.

In terms of my happiest moments as a mother, I think of a time when my daughter was about nine, and I got a Jeep. I really wanted a Jeep. I'd finished my studying and I was expressing myself more as an individual at that time. That was a momentous thing for me that she shared and thought was wonderful. Heidi and I drove in that Jeep across country. We were in the process of moving back to New York, and we chose to do it in this Jeep with the soft top and the flaps down. We went to the Grand Canyon and stopped in Santa Fe and went up to Colorado and had the grandest adventure. We were like friends. I couldn't believe that I was doing something so independent and exciting, and she somehow made me feel strong and capable through her friendship and the partnership we had.

I had the great benefit of having a daughter who was

always very caring and sweet. There's no question that I consider motherhood to be joyous. No question that it's one of the most fulfilling events of my life.

Elizabeth Colton

Philanthropist/Women's Advocate

– Mother of 2 –

Motherhood can be both joyous and torturous at the same time. Sometimes motherhood absolutely provides great moments of joy. Those could be from the simple acts of laughing and playing with your kids, or exploring and discovering new things together on a hike or on a trip. Happiness can also come from more profound things, like a breakthrough moment when they all of a sudden start doing well in school, or they can all of a sudden jump the four-foot fence or achieve something that they've been working hard at. Certainly the traditional moments of pride, graduations, and those kinds of things are great joys because you see that your child has successfully made it through another stage in life.

I also find a sense of joy and satisfaction when you see them reflecting back the values that you tried to teach them. That can be one of the most rewarding times. Again, it's mixed and there are a lot of frustrating, difficult times. You have to be patient with those times as well as know how to recognize and enjoy the joyful ones.

Gretchen DeWitt

Public Relations

– Mother of 2 –

The happiest moments with my mother were the many

times we went to the beach and she painted her toenails while I floated away on a yellow raft. And Christmas—though I thought it was Santa, it was really my mother. I always loved the 5 a.m. surprise under the Christmas tree. I loved Thanksgiving. I loved costumes she found for me for Halloween. And I loved Easter egg hunts at Easter. I loved watching my mother be amusing and kind and generous.

As far as the happiest part of being a mother, it was really the immediate moments after giving birth and those first few times with a new baby. That was such fulfillment. I felt like I'd run a marathon and had gotten the big prize.

After that, the moments that I loved most were really echoes of the moments I loved about my mother. I liked doing the same things my mother had done for me.

Tricia LaVoice

Psychologist/Stay-at-Home Mom

– Mother of 4 –

I would say the best week of my life would probably be the week that I gave birth and my mother came and stayed with me. When I was pregnant with my daughter, one of my friend's mothers had said that infants were for women. I found that offensive, and I really wanted my husband to be part of the birth and the first week after. But when the baby came, truly as much as I love my husband to death, I wanted him to go to work and to share that experience with my mother. It was just the best week of being a mother because it was all so new and I had this big, beautiful baby girl. Everything was perfect, and my mother was there, and she was so proud. She said, "Who loves your babies as much as you? The only people who love your babies as much as you are your mother and your husband." So that would absolutely be the best week.

Stacy Friedman

Rabbi

– Mother of 2 –

My happiest moments with my children are those small moments. They are not necessarily the planned theme park moments or things like that, but the small moments. Last night I put my son to sleep. I said, "Adam, I have to kiss you one hundred times before you go to sleep," and he had the biggest smile on his face. I said to him and to my other son, "You are my two most precious possessions in the world. Now I've got to go downstairs and go to sleep." He said, "But, Mommy, how will you watch over your precious possessions if you're downstairs?" We just started giggling and having fun. So as a mother the joyous moments are those sweet moments that just happen when you're not expecting them.

Being a mother is definitely joyous, and I think it's important to have that joy to balance the great responsibility of raising children. I remember to make sure to sprinkle the day with joy and fun and good humor. One of the things that my mother taught me, because there were difficult times in her life growing up as a child, was to laugh at things. When she would get the dishes out of the cabinet, she had this little joke about being up above the world so high. She would never just take a dish down—it became a song and a dance every time we would do something like that. Or every month we used to have utensil night, when you couldn't use silverware. You had to use other utensils, just for the moment of creating, for the purpose of creating joy.

I think it's important to tap into that natural joy. It reminds us that that the things we worry about are not so important. Sometimes we get caught up with our kids' performance or how they're doing or whether they're doing what they need to be doing. All those things in the long run really don't matter. What matters is the joy and the love we have. They remember that, and then they remember a happy childhood.

Sharon Cohn

Entrepreneur

– Mother of 4 –

I've been a daughter for forty-six years with an incredible mother. I have two daughters, who are eighteen and twenty-one, and two stepsons, who are twenty-nine and twenty-seven. I am so thankful I was able to have the experience of being a mom. It's not going to go away, it just changes. I couldn't imagine having a life without it.

I enjoyed so much being a part of my children's lives. They were very sports-minded. One was a competitive swimmer and the other an equestrian. Just being able to experience their joy of doing those things is so important to me. It was so important to be there, even if it meant getting up at 4 a.m. to get them to swim practice before school and getting them there afterward, and trying to fit it all in. It was what made them happy, and I was so honored to be a part of that. That was very special to me. And just the hugs and the unconditional love that you get from them. Because no matter how you try, you're going to make mistakes, but they always love you and having that love back keeps you going.

Amy Apollo Ahumada

Boutique Manager

– Mother of 2 –

My mom and I are best friends, so I have countless memories with her. I consider her my advisor, my best friend, my counsel, my support. I mean she's everything to me. She's hilarious and makes me laugh. She is fun to laugh with, fun to eat with, fun to talk to, fun to watch movies with. We both love getting a box of Kleenex and crying together in movies. We love calling each other just to share anything, even if it's mundane. We talk all the time.

My children are so much fun. We have fun singing together and dancing together and building zoos together with blocks and animals and learning Origami together and reading stories. Reading to my kids is probably my favorite time of the day. It's very special. We do it every single night. We read before nap-times. Those times are really precious moments for me.

I'm a mom who doesn't sit at the park with a latte in my hand. I'm on the playground, playing with my kids. I like roller-skating and ice skating and skateboarding and playing Play Station 2 with them. I just enjoy them thoroughly. It is what I always dreamed of being when I was a child. I feel like if I die tomorrow I will have lived a full life because I got to be a mother.

Barbara Rosenberg

Community Volunteer/Philanthropist

– Mother of 2 –

I have an older brother who asked me, "What was the happiest day you ever spent with Mom?" I said I couldn't really think of one. I'm not saying that in a sad way. I think that there were more obligatory things that were required of us growing up, like going to school, achieving, doing well in school. I was a child of the Depression, and what you didn't have materially you made up for educationally, you made up for by achievement, by knowledge, by bearing a good name for the family. So the girly things that were so wonderful about a mother-daughter relationship just didn't exist.

I think that more joyous memories were when my mother was older and I began to play the role of the mother and she the child. She lived in San Francisco at the Jewish Home. My father died in his early seventies of leukemia. We thought my mother would fall apart, but she was very strong, and she knew when she needed help. When she came to San Francisco and was living at the Jewish Home, we became quite close. Perhaps I had grown a lot, perhaps she was less rigid and more relaxed, but there were some very happy memories. She was very outgoing, very joyful, and very happy to be in her environment.

With my own children, there's a sense of great pride. We have one son who's doing a youth summer camp for underprivileged children in Los Angeles. These are inner-city kids. He has gotten the city to underwrite the insurance for several parks over the summer, and he provides all of the counselors, the mentors, and the programs for these kids. There's a great source of pride that the notion of *tikunolam*, which among Jews is a commandment to mend a broken world, is something that we successfully seem to have passed to our children.

The younger son, Peter, is active at the Jewish Home, where his grandmothers lived. He's on the board. He's active in the Living Legacy Society of the Jewish Community

Federation. He and his wife both volunteer at their children's school. So it thrills me to see the next generation. Another aspect of Jewish life is also "the door of the door." What we do is from generation to generation. That's a very important theme in our life. Everything you do should be an example for the next generation.

Carol Bartz

Entrepreneur

– Mother of 1 –

*M*otherhood is the most fulfilling thing in your lifetime. It can give you the biggest joy, but it can also give you the biggest sorrow. It's a double-edged sword with an amazing emotional range. I don't think there is a love that matches the love for a child. The unique intensity of it feels very different from any other kind of love that you can experience. It's perfection. Nothing else in this world can tweak you as much as what a child can do, both positive and negative. The understanding of that is absolutely essential so that you can stay sane in the middle somewhere, especially at a time when my daughter is now asking whether she can get that fifth hole in her ear, after she didn't tell me about the third and fourth ones.

I would like to say that the happiest moments are always yet to come. I'm not one who thinks that I've already had the happiest something. This is just a wonderful journey you're on. I hate the prom queen deal, which is, gee, the happiest moment in my life was when I was a prom queen. Well, you know, you have sixty more years to live after that, honey. I just think there are so many happy moments it's a shame to pull out a happiest one.

Mary Poland

Philanthropist/Stay-at-Home Mom

– Mother of 1 –

With my mother it was just mundane things that were the happiest things. It's the shopping together, being in the kitchen, or talking about my disappointments. Maybe there were some kids that were mean to me in junior high. I could talk to her, and she would always make me feel good. I don't know exactly what she said, but I could tell that she cared and that she knew I was working as hard as I could and that she was there to support me and protect me if I needed that. And that stayed with me.

My mother's touch meant a lot to me. She could put her hands through my hair, and I would feel so good. I don't forget to do that for my own son even though he's thirteen now. I still feel touch is so important. I make a point every day of touching or holding him or tousling his hair. I think that human touch is necessary. The words are important, but actions speak louder than words.

The highlight for Stratton and me is the everyday rhythm of life. Every day I go down to the school and see him. I try to blend into the walls down there so nobody really sees me. Seeing him interact with the children and seeing him slowly maturing is such a heartfelt feeling. Every day is like a miracle, a gift from God.

Arlene Ackerman

School Superintendent

– Mother of 2 –

As far as my mother is concerned, I became closer to her when I became a mother. I valued her wisdom. I valued the things that she did with us that I had taken for granted, the sacrifices she made. As I became a mother I really appreciated her more, and I found myself calling her for advice.

My mother passed away almost five years ago now. Her passing was probably one of the hardest things for me to accept. Whenever I think about her, I'm happy. I feel I was so lucky to have her as a mother, and I wish I'd spent more time telling her that. I wish I had spent more time giving back to her. I just took for granted that she'd be around a long time and I'd be able to do that. Her passing has helped me focus and refocus my attention again to the gift of being a mother and connecting with my children more. I wouldn't want to look back and say I wish I'd spent more time with them or I wish I connected with them more. I probably call them much more than they would like to hear me calling, but when they don't hear from me for a few days they call me. So I think they kind of like it even though they complain.

There are a lot of great memories that I have with my children. One story comes to mind. My boys were about eight and five, and Mother's Day was coming up. At that time I was a single parent. They'd saved their money and they went out to get me a present. They came back, and they were very secretive. They said I couldn't see this present until Mother's Day. They assured me every day that I was absolutely going to love this present. It was the best present they'd ever given me.

Mother's Day came, and they brought in this present,

and it's all wrapped up. It was a scarf with nothing but horse heads on it. It was absolutely the ugliest thing I've ever seen in my life. I was horrified that they gave me this. And they said, "Isn't it the greatest? Isn't it the greatest scarf you've ever seen?" I knew they bought it at a flea market or something, or one of the garage sales, and they were so happy with it.

I still have that horse-head scarf. Every once in a while I'll take it out and I'll smile. It's not a big deal, but I knew that gift came from their heart. I knew that it gave them pleasure to give it to me, and as a result I treasure this scarf, which is absolutely the most hideous thing you've ever seen. But that's certainly one of my happiest moments.

Donna Radu
Equity Trader/Stay-at-Home Mom
– Mother of 2 –

The happiest moments I spent with my mom were when we were doing things together, when I watched her express herself. My mother had a beautiful voice. She sang to us once in a while. We always had music in the house, and I remember she'd all of a sudden boom into a song, and it was so beautiful to watch. It just made me smile. All my mother did was take care of us and cook and clean, and I didn't get a chance very often to see her do that for her. So those are great moments.

I remember, too, baking apple pies in the kitchen, having her teach us how to do that and actually working side by side with her. She was so patient and so loving. Those were great moments as a little girl.

When I grew up and I was working in my twenties, my mom would come into the city. She'd come downtown and have lunch and spend time with me, go dancing. She became more of a friend. It was great because we were close. We'd go to fashion shows once in a while. It was just being with her by myself.

Raising Jameson and Brandon has given me a greater purpose. You give them life, but they give you life every day. They change every day. They are a tremendous amount of work, and I'm exhausted most of the time, but I love it. I love everything they do. I love watching them. I can't wait to go in and wake them up in the morning. When they interact with other children or other people, it's a thrill for me. Sometimes when I drop one of them off at preschool, I stand in the wings or behind the door and just watch them. I could do that all day. It's so awesome to watch the way they develop and grow into their own little personalities. I love that. They give you so much more back.

Ariel Bybee

Mezzo-Soprano/Voice Teacher

– Mother of 1 –

I think the happiest moments are the little ones. My daughter is a pianist, and some of the happiest moments we have are making music together. She plays piano and I sing, and there's a creative process that takes place. We make music in a similar way, so we have such a great bonding when we make music together. That's a lot of fun. I think I'm lucky, though. I had a daughter that I called PPC—practically perfect child. She never caused any problems. Even during her teenage years, she was Little Miss Perfect. So the moments I've shared with her have definitely been joyous. I haven't received any greater joy in my life from anybody.

Chapter 4

A Mother's Instinct and Intuition

*It's very important to be in touch with our
primitive personas. These intuitions are there
to help us. We need to listen very carefully
to what they are telling us, because
they usually are correct.*

GRETCHEN DeWITT

People often speak of maternal instinct and a mother's intuition. Are instinct and intuition real? What role do they play in a mother's life?

Instinct is an inborn, natural impulse to behave in a way that is characteristic of a species. Throughout the animal kingdom, the maternal instinct serves to protect the young from predators and ensure survival. Intuition is insight or knowledge without reasoning or analysis: a hunch, in other words. When we act on a "feeling" that cannot be rationally explained, are we acting on faith or some sort of pre-verbal knowledge? The source and validity of these feelings may certainly be debated.

Some of the women represented in this chapter believe that instinct and intuition are "hard-wired" into us as mothers, while others think they can be learned and cultivated. Many point to the importance of simply paying attention. All, however, affirm the importance of having confidence in the inner voice that speaks to us.

Carmel Greenwood

Author/Entrepreneur/Lecturer

– Mother of 5 –

For me, maternal instinct and intuition have played a very important role. My eldest son had his twenty-first birthday, and I had a nightmare that night that he'd overdosed. He turned blue and the ambulance came. It was so strong that I woke up in a cold sweat. When I phoned my son and daughter the next day, they said they had a wonderful party, nothing was wrong. But my maternal instinct knew there was something wrong. I hopped on a plane from Hong Kong and went to Australia, and, sure enough, he'd been injecting heroine and had overdosed that night. So maternal instinct is always correct. No matter where I am in the world, I can tune in to my children and see what's going on. They all know I've got eyes in the back of my head.

I think as women we're very tuned in to our intuition, and I've learned to follow that implicitly now.

Isabel Allende

Author

– Mother of 2 –

As a mother you develop certain abilities when it's required. We women have to take care of the children, so we have a third eye in the back of our head to see what every child is doing at any given time while we are doing other things. I think that that is what we call intuition—the capacity to observe details that are necessary and that most people don't have the need to observe. A mother knows without touching a child if the child is feverish, if the child is hungry, if the child is lying. I know when one of my grandchildren is lying without looking at the child's face. Just an intonation, experience, intuition, I don't know what it is. Mostly it's because we mothers observe very carefully.

Virginia Harris
Spiritual Leader
– Mother of 3 –

Intuition is one of women's greatest assets. We've been cultivating it for centuries, for millennia. I think we've been cultivating it because we haven't been able to speak. It made us program ourselves to listen, listen, listen.

Women have developed a very keen sense of reading and knowing a situation. They have the ability to see and hear sometimes beyond what appears on the surface, to feel intuitively what is right or what's the next thing to do before we see the facts and know the right things to do.

Our intuition, our maternal instinct, is that radar antenna that guides us, that knows when to move, knows when to do this or do that. It brings a sense of wisdom and poise and peace, but it has to be cultivated. We crowd it out if we don't allow ourselves to have that mental space to truly listen. I make space every morning and every evening to just sit and be still because I feel that nurtures me and cultivates and develops that spiritual listening. It's when I stop talking, it's when I stop mentally processing and reasoning and truly listen. Listen to the thoughts; listen to the angels that are whispering.

I used to feel that with the children. I would sometimes know things before they called. I often knew before they knew, and they'd say, "Mother, how did you know that?" "Oh, mother has eyes all over her head. Ears all over her face." They would laugh.

We almost know not only what the bodies of our children are feeling but also the bodies of our family, the bodies of our community. I certainly rely on it in my own life today, in the boardroom, in different places. It's an important quality that's needed not just at the kitchen table but at the board table, the bedside, the lawyer's bench, the negotiating and peace table. Spiritual intuition, intuition, maternal instinct—whatever we call it, it's something that is very, very precious, and it needs to be valued because it's spiritual equipment that God has given us to get through the day.

Jennifer Morla

Entrepreneur/Designer

– Mother of 2 –

I believe maternal instinct is hardwired in us. I don't think I could have even identified that prior to having the children. It is there, and I guess it's maybe even hard for me to isolate what is just life experience, and what is maternal instinct.

I remember when they were just learning how to walk, and if there was a box top on the floor, the newspapers, whatever, they would step on top of everything. You say, "You know, you're going to break that." You're immediate thought is, why are you stepping on top of that? Why don't you just go around it? And then, for a flash, I remembered what it was to feel the difference of texture underneath your feet. There was that tactile feeling that I remembered, in some very primal way, that made me think, that's why they're doing that. That's what you're constantly doing as a mom or parent, I'm sure. You are just remembering back, it brings you back to that point, and you remember why you did what you did. Then you get to see it through their eyes.

There is that immense caring all the time, and trying to look ahead and get rid of whatever obstacles there could be. I think part of my role is not to tell them what that road is, but to try and alleviate any obstacles that could let them find that road. It's hard making those right choices, even counseling them and talking to them. I think part of the challenge of being a mother is trying to remember that they don't always need advice. As a mother, you try to fix things. Sometimes they need to fix it themselves.

That is just intense. Even the smallest thing—so-and-so didn't play with me today. You want to react, but I stay back. The teachers love me, because there's a certain point where I say, this is your realm and you can do this. Unless I see some big issue, I'm going to stay out of the picture. I'm going to be involved, but I'm not going to intervene.

And that's hard. It's wrenching, really, because you feel their pain. My sister had to have an operation when she was around thirteen, and I remember my mother saying, "Oh, I wish I were going into this operation, and not her." Of course, I didn't understand. Why would you want to go through this? And, of course, as a mother, you'd let a train run over you.

Judith Epstein

Appellate Judge

– Mother of 2 –

I have my own view of maternal instinct and intuition, and that's because, in my family situation, it was shared fifty-fifty with my husband, who I felt had demonstrated every bit as much maternal instinct and intuition as I did. In fact, when you put the two of us together, you get one good mother. I think it's partly because of who he is and partly because we started on this adventure so early in our own formative years, so that neither one of us had any preconceived notion of what mothering roles involved, what mothering itself involved. His own instincts led him to step into the void so quickly and so early on, and he did it so well, that it was really a shared experience. My husband had every bit as much of a nurturing and parenting instinct as I did. In fact, when we separated from the children, he had a much greater separation anxiety than I did.

It is still rare to see a male who has a true mothering instinct, even though men are taking on a more affirmative parenting role. In this instance, the indefinable mothering instinct that, I think, most women who are mothers would understand, is one that my husband also had. He's a very manly man, but he certainly had it.

Laurel Biever

Counselor/Therapist

– Mother of 1 –

Nothing could have ever prepared me for the amount of love and awe and protective nature that happened instantaneously when I had my daughter. In that moment when she was born, when I looked at her and held her, there was just a physical reaction that happened inside of me. I knew I could do and would do whatever it took to be there for her and raise her in the most wonderful way I could. That's a really hard thing to describe. It was a very sobering moment, just the intensity that I felt. I think part of that is maternal instinct.

It's one of those things where you completely get outside of yourself. Your personal things don't matter in that moment. It's this drive to do and say and be whatever you need to be in order to make them know that you're there and that they're safe and you'll be there for them.

Yasmine Ahmed McGrane
Entrepreneur
– Future mother –

I think if you have an open heart, if you really try and listen to what your heart is directing you to do, then you can make some really good decisions. My mother pretty much raised three children by intuition. For the first eight years of my life, my father was working in the States, and my mother raised the three children in Canada completely on her own. That's a lot. I think having one child is like having two corporate careers. And she didn't have any teachers, mentors, or books to read. She did it all through intuition. It's just all relating to your children as the being that you are. Not putting up pretenses. Not making your children afraid of you. Just making it simple. Getting down to the core of why you chose to have children for the joy of it.

Alexia Nye Jackson
Comedienne/Stay-at-Home Mom
– Mother of 3 –

A mother's maternal instinct and intuition relate to my experience a great deal. Some women have it more than others, but I do think there's certainly a process that happens in the months of carrying your child. I'm sure there are certain things that happen physiologically, that nature takes care of itself and you start to prepare in that way. But beyond that, it's an incredibly powerful thing to want to protect and nurture your child and the lengths that you go to do that.

I think that's why the journey of mothering is so important and so huge. You become a giver, and you become a person who wants to impart knowledge. You want to explain to somebody how to do something a little bit better than they might be doing it or exactly how to pour this particular liquid or how to fold the clothes or how to do things with grace and integrity. I think women have a fuller sense of that.

There have been other things that have happened in terms of endangerment with my children. One time my littlest one had gone around the fence to the edge of our swimming pool. I was in the middle of a conversation with my dad out on the front deck. I didn't hear a thing, and I had absolutely no reason to get up, but I said "Just a minute." I walked to the end of the deck and looked down the side of the house and down that narrow path, and there was Brady standing at the deep end, throwing rocks into the pool. I don't know to this day why I did that. How did I know to go do that? I just feel like you are connected to your children all the time. You just know where their person is, where their energy is, what's happening with them. That's one of the stories that moved me to follow a maternal instinct, follow an intuition about my connection with my child.

Elizabeth Colton

Philanthropist/Women's Advocate

– Mother of 2 –

I think this is something that changes at different stages in your child's growth. When your child is a newborn baby, it's pretty strong and clear that most maternal instinct is to care for the child, to hold the child, to nurture it, feed it. Sometimes you have to learn how to do those things. But most of us have no training and yet can slide right into that role because of a certain instinct about how to be nurturing and how to take care of your child as a baby.

It gets less clear as your children get older. You might have certain instincts about whether or not you should let your child do a certain activity. You might have some instincts about whether or not their current group of friends is a positive group for them to be in. You might have instincts about what would be a good course for your child to take. But as the child gets older and older, you have to balance more and more your instincts with your own child's needs. As your child's identity is growing, those two become more separate. Hopefully they work together, but sometimes you have to rely a little less on your maternal instincts as your kids get older. But there will always be a time when you may just know that your child needs you a little more. Children need you to give them a hug and say it's all right. And that can happen at any age.

Gretchen DeWitt

Public Relations

– Mother of 2 –

I think it's important to listen to our intuition, to those intuitive feelings. Our gut response is about 90 percent accurate and then we tend to intellectualize and talk ourselves out of what we felt was the truth because it isn't something desirable or convenient for us to believe. There were times when I thought something dangerous was going on and was reassured by a daughter that it wasn't. And in fact my intuition was correct. So I think it's very important to be in touch with our primitive personas. These intuitions are there to help us. We need to listen very carefully to what they are telling us, because they usually are correct. When my daughter was fifteen I had a feeling that she was on drugs. I asked her, based on her angry, erratic behavior, if she was and if she needed help. She laughed merrily and told me I was crazy. Because I wanted to believe that there wasn't a problem, I disregarded my intuition. Years later she told me she had been addicted to cocaine for a year in high school. I learned a lesson that time and many other times. We need to train ourselves to pay careful attention to our intuitive selves.

Tricia LaVoice

Psychologist/Stay-at-Home Mom

– Mother of 4 –

*A*lthough I really had my head in a place to be a career woman, when I started having babies, everybody teased that

I finally got the job I wanted. For me it all came very instinctually because I'd been babysitting and playing with babies. However, one of my best friends, Sheila, probably never thought about motherhood until the day her baby came home. The first couple of months that she was a mother, she didn't know what to do. I was very close with her, talking all the time, and I watched her study motherhood, get books, and talk. She developed this instinct to the point that I call her and go at it with her about mothering. She's an incredible mother. Without my experience with Sheila, I don't know whether I would think that you could ever develop mother instincts, because for me it was so natural. Now I look at her, and she's so maternal, so instinctual. I would say to any woman who didn't feel very maternal instinctually that it comes and it can develop.

Jeannie Brown

Entrepreneur

– Mother of 3 –

When you are growing up, you have all of these different experiences. So you know when your child is having an experience. You have the intuition, "Oh my goodness, my daughter is growing up, she's thirteen years old. This is happening to her." "Oh my goodness, my daughter is sixteen, she's having her first love affair." I could tell you without her saying one word to me what she was going through. If she and her boyfriend had a fight, I knew it before she ever told me. I've been through it all, so I see it in my children when they have these emotional strains.

Stacy Friedman

Rabbi

– Mother of 2 –

*I*ntuition is so much a part of mothering, and yet so much of what the world and our culture feed us today is counter-intuitive. We have all these books about how to raise your children, and all these advice shows and talk shows and people telling you what to do. I think we're really lacking trust in ourselves, that people really doubt their instincts. I know I do sometimes. I think it's important to get in touch with that, when you take your child to the doctor to say, "You know what, I know something." This happened to me a couple of weeks ago. My child's sick. Why? He didn't eat three eggs today, he only had one, and he looked at me funny. I said, "He's sick and he has strep throat." You just know these things. Whether that's instinct or paying atten-tion, I don't know, but I think that it's important to be in touch with that.

It also teaches us how to be instinctual about the rest of our lives and how to really pay attention. I think being a mother helps us to pay attention to the rest of our lives because we need to pay attention to our children, and they feel the difference. My son feels so light and happy when I notice things or pay attention. He says, Mommy, you brought me my favorite whatever it is. And how do you know what those are? Partly it's just paying attention.

Benita Potters

Entrepreneur/Community Volunteer

– Mother of 2 –

A mother's instinct is so strong, you've got to listen to that. It's that spirit that knows when something's wrong and when something's working, too. I used it much more often in knowing that what I was being told wasn't perhaps the God's honest truth or that there was something funny going on. I swear I could tell my kids were going to get sick before they were sick. It was just a weird thing. I can't read anybody else like that. So I think mother's instinct works, and that it's incredibly important to listen to it.

Sharon Cohn

Entrepreneur

– Mother of 4 –

There's no instruction book that comes with children when they're born. In my experience, there's a sense of what you want and how you want it to be, remembering how your mother did it, remembering how other women in your life did it, and remembering your friend's moms who did it. And then you start in.

For me, a lot of it had to do with my mom being there and just saying "Trust yourself" and "You can do it." I think that's the encouragement every new mother needs. You just have to trust that you're going to be able to take care of whatever needs to be taken care of and create the world for your child that you want to create. Think about what that is, and go for that.

Sylvia Boorstein

Author/Buddhist Teacher

– Mother of 4 –

Today there are a million baby books that tell you something about everything. As well as parents' magazines and baby magazines. There's so much information out there. There was none of that when my children were born. There was Dr. Spock, and there was a little book written by a British psychoanalyst, David Winnicott. In his book Winnicott said, you're the child's mother; you'll know what to do. My Spock book told me, feed now, do this, do that, do the other, and this book said to me, you're going to know what your child needs because you're his mother. I found that so consoling. Many a night when an infant was crying and I was at my wits' end, I thought to myself, I know what to do, this is my child. Maybe the book said don't feed the child every time that it wants to eat, let it cry and let it cry itself to sleep. I said, "I'm not doing that." So it was very consoling to have Winnicott say, you are the child's mother. You know what to do.

Amy Apollo Ahumada

Boutique Manager

– Mother of 2 –

I think it's really hard because I know that sometimes I can be too overprotective or worry too much about my kids. I think your maternal instinct sometimes can blur with just being worried.

There have been times where I've been confused about whether something is a real intuition or whether I'm just nervous about whatever the situation is. Oh, my son's going on his first sleepover. Okay, wait. Am I getting this feeling because something has happened and I should call him and check on him right now? My intuition and gut feelings have saved me from many traumas time and time again, so I listen very carefully to them and take them very seriously. When it comes to my kids, though, I just have to check and make sure it really is my maternal instinct and not just my being nervous or worried right now.

Gretchen de Baubigny

Community Volunteer/Consultant

– Mother of 2 –

*I*t is so interesting how you know when your child is sick. You can be in a sound sleep, and you hear the cry. As adults my children can be in New York on the phone, and I say, "What's wrong?" Although the conversation tries to be light-hearted, I know that underneath something is going on.

Then there's also the instinct of the children for their parent. One day I had a terrible accident. I fell down the stairs right here in front of our house, and my elbow went into my liver area. I cut my liver all the way across and had centimeters or millimeters on either edge keeping me together. I broke my teeth and did all kinds of things. My daughter was stepping off a curb in New York and she said, "Something's happening to my mother." So that very morning she was aware of something.

I love the honesty with my children, not only verbally but also instinctively. We understand one another's joys and more deeply, of course, one another's pain. You understand the pain and you know. I think my children know there is a mom there who is on their side forever.

Barbara Rosenberg

Community Volunteer/Philanthropist

– Mother of 2 –

Maternal instinct is a much overused expression. Some people have it, some people don't. I would rather use "instinct" than "maternal instinct." Sometimes maternal instinct is mistaken for your pattern of living, your practice of living. A kid normally comes home from school at two o'clock. He's not there until three. The pattern is broken and an intelligent person will say, "Look, there's something wrong here." I think sometimes the living patterns will prompt what we call instinct rather than common sense.

Some people just don't have that. They don't connect the dots. You can't say it's motherly instinct. Fathers have it, aunts have it, uncles have it, friends have it. It's a sense of being able to read other people and also being able to predict. And that relates to also to intuition. Again, some people have a greater sense of intuition than others. Men have instinct and intuition just as women do.

Carol Bartz

Entrepreneur

– Mother of 1 –

I have the advantage of being one type of person before forty and a different person after. If I had been a mom at twenty, I'm not sure that I could have totally understood myself in this way. Actually, I don't think I had any maternal instincts. I was a nice person, but I never tried to pick up babies. I never goo-gooed and carried on. When people

tried to give them to me, I'd say, "No, that's okay." I completely flip-flopped on that, completely became fascinated
with children and very protective of them.

I remember one time sitting in the car with my daughter, Laney. She would have been four or five at the time. My
husband was getting pizza, and another mother got out of her
car and jerked her kid's arm, almost pulled this kid's arm
out. She was berating him and carrying on, and Laney and I
were watching this together. I finally turned to her and said,
"That's not a very good mom." You wanted to jump out and
shake this mother and say, "Oh my God, why would you do
that? There's no reason to do that." I think before I would
have looked at that curiously and probably felt it was terrible
for her to do, but it wouldn't have pulled at my heartstrings
the way it did actually watching that with my daughter.

Mary Poland
Philanthropist/Stay-at-Home Mom
– Mother of 1 –

I guess I'm like a mother bear. I'm very protective of my
cub. I've always had a good intuition on a lot of fronts and
a sixth sense. I've taken that talent, if you will, and put that
into the mothering aspects with my son. I also take my life
experiences. I make a conscious effort of thinking what I
would be like at thirteen. I think about feelings and emotions, teacher relationships, how teachers would relate to me
and what they would say to me to make me excel or be moti-
vated or just rain on my parade.

One of the things I do is I try to read the non-verbal
cues a lot, especially when I pick him up from school. I look
at his face and it's a challenge to me to say, did he have a

good day, did he have a bad day? Can I tell with the eyes, whether they're sparkly, or from his posture? So that's part of the intuition that I try to hone in on. It's important.

As they get older, boys may not be as verbal with you. They go through phases. It can be good, it can be bad. The important thing is that, when they do talk to you about the most mundane thing in the world and you are in the middle of a few other fires on the burners and your life is going on, you stop that life and you listen to whatever silly subject he's talking about. Usually with my son it's an observation. He has tons of observations about things right now. You're thinking, I already know this one, I know the answer to this observation. I've been there a thousand times, and I'm having to listen to it like it's brand new. But you stop and you listen to it. You just bite the inside of your mouth and you say, "That's very fascinating that you thought about it like that." Whatever the subject, you stop in your tracks, and it might as well be he's telling you that he's discovered a cure for cancer.

Arlene Ackerman

School Superintendent

– Mother of 2 –

My mom always knew in the first two words if something was wrong. I think that was a mother's instinct. She would know if it was something good I was calling about or if it was something that I was upset about or sad about.

I feel I could do the same thing with my boys. When they call me, I can tell when they say "Hi, Mom," how that conversation is going to move. There's a red light or flashing light that says slow down, listen, something's coming up and either prepare to support or prepare to celebrate. Sometimes I just know when I need to call one of my sons, and I call, and it's the right time. "Oh, Mom, I'm so glad you called." I can't tell you how many times that's happened. I can't tell you why I got up out of a meeting and came in and called, but I just felt at that time that my children needed me. I listened to it. When I hear a small voice that talks to me, I act on it right away. I've never been sorry that I did, and I've never really been wrong. Either it's going to be something great, or it's going to be that they need some kind of emotional support or financial support, but it's something.

My grandmother said that when children are young they're on your lap, but when they're older they're in your heart. I feel that about motherhood, too. They stay with you whether they're physically there or in your heart.

Chapter 5

A Mother's Work

*So long as you believe that you are giving your
children what they need to be healthy, happy
individuals, you're doing a good job. . . . One can
be the fullest person inside, offer the most love
to the child, or not. The only right way is
what is right for the individual.*

YASMINE AHMED MCGRANE

A mother's work—giving life and caring for a child—is
uniquely challenging and immensely rewarding. Yet it is terribly undervalued in our society.

This lack of recognition of motherhood as invaluable
work contributes to a common conundrum: the decision to
be either a working mom or a stay-at-home mom. For many
mothers, there is no choice at all—they must work outside
the home to support their families. But others struggle with
this painful decision. Whatever they decide, all mothers
experience conflicting emotions as they balance their own
needs and ambitions against their desire to be a great mom.

The experiences and insights in this chapter offer
encouragement to all mothers. These women stress that
working outside the home need not impair one's ability to
mother successfully. Several describe how their careers and
their motherhood have actually enhanced each other. The

general consensus is that all mothers are working moms, whether they work outside the home or not.

As human beings, we are all inherently fallible. Letting go of the illusion of being the perfect mother is vital to finding the right balance. These women emphasize that the best mother is a happy mother. In the end, each of us must find our own path, so long as we give our children the love and attention they need to thrive.

Isabel Allende

Author

– Mother of 2 –

When I think of those moments that have marked my destiny and changed my life completely, undoubtedly giving birth was one of those moments. But I don't think that it is the most important work that every single woman does. Giving birth is important, caring for children is important, but there are women who have many other things to do that are just as important as caring for children—discovering things, going to places, writing, other things. It's not as if because we don't have a child we are not contributing to the world.

I wish I could have been a mom who stayed at home the first few years of my children's life, because I think that it probably would have been better for them. I was lucky—I had a mother-in-law who lived close by, and she was very present, so she helped me. I couldn't stay at home, because I was bored to death. I thought that caring for a child was like going back to childhood. Talking like a child, being aware only of primal necessities and primal needs of the child—there was no intellectual life, no other things that I wanted to do.

So I could never stay at home. But if someone can do it, and likes to do it, I think it's the best thing. Society should make that possible. Mothers should be paid to stay at home, as they are in France and many other places. If that's the best for the child and they want to do it, it's not fair that they have to go and work.

It's like teachers. Nobody recognizes how important they are in the society until they are not there.

Virginia Harris
Spiritual Leader
– Mother of 3 –

Giving life and caring for a child are very, very important. Is it the most important work I will ever do? If you had asked me that question twenty-five years ago, when I was in the throes of raising the boys, I would have said yes, it's absolutely the most important work I will ever do. But now, with a little longer view on it, I've seen how I have now put those qualities that I felt were so important in the moments of three little boys into other aspects of my life, into a broader sense of family and community and society. I've seen that I'm developing and nurturing and helping guide not just little boys and little girls, but ideas and organizations and very, very dear needs in the world.

When my children were young, I was very involved in the prevention of child abuse and neglect in the community. It was in the mid-seventies, when this was not something that's talked about like it is today. I had three little boys at home, and our home was always the center of activity. Every day I baked. I baked chocolate chip cookies one day and pumpkin bread the next and peanut butter cookies the next. So there was always something in the afternoons that smelled good coming from our kitchen. The little neighbor-hood boys would come in and they'd put their fingers in the cookie dough batter, or they'd eat it warm out of the oven, and they always would gravitate to our home. When I began to work in the community in the prevention of child abuse and neglect, my idealistic thought was if I could scoop up all the children that are abused in the world and bring them to my kitchen for a couple of afternoons, maybe I could solve all the world's problems. I realized that I'd been given the opportunity to take those qualities of mothering and nurtur-ing into that broader family of community and society. My desire to do that as a young mother, and my community work with my own children, led me into the career of help-ing emotionally and physically ill and wounded people get better, helping others on their spiritual journey. I'm grateful that I've been able to take those qualities and help others, whether individuals or organizations, grow and develop.

I have been both a working mom and a stay-at-home mom. There are advantages and disadvantages, challenges and opportunities. I think that every mother is a working mother. Every mother is an executive. Every mother is a manager. Every mother is a leader. Every mother is a custo-dian. We're all of these things in one.

I'm grateful that I have the choice, and I'm grateful that there isn't the pressure either from society or for other rea-sons to say that one is right or one is not right. Ten, fifteen years ago, if you stayed at home, that was demoralizing. That wasn't going to get you anywhere. Now today, we've got lots of mothers opting out of boardrooms to stay at home. It's a choice. I think as long as people are honest, it's okay. Just do it your way and enjoy it. Love who you are this moment. Do what is best for your family and your children.

Judith Epstein

Appellate Judge

– Mother of 2 –

Each mother owes it to her children, since she brought them into this world, to try to give them the best mother that she can be, without putting impossible standards on herself. Some women feel that the way they can be the best mom is to be a stay-at-home mom, and some women feel that the way they can be the best mom is to seek out other avenues of developing their individuality. To me, it depends on what it is they need as individuals to make themselves strong and able to be a good person and, therefore, a good mother. Most moms don't have a choice, and it would be cruel to punish them by saying there's a best and a worse way. I don't think there is really a best way. There's only a way.

Young mothers need to know that no matter what the choice—whether they stay at home, or they choose to work, or they must work and they also choose to have a family—either decision is full of enormous stresses, and enormous questions of self-doubt. None of us can walk down a straight path and say, this is the right way. Every day presents a question of what is the best way to do something, and often it's not apparent until after you've either made the choice and it's a mistake or made the choice and it's a success.

In the early days with my children, I made enormous efforts to balance the time commitment of my career with the amount of time I wanted to spend with my family. I chose, basically, to give those two my focus, and nothing else. We had very little social life other than that of the family. When my daughter was young, she would ask me why I couldn't be a real mother like other neighborhood mothers. She had a perception that she was being short-changed. She now says, as an adult, that she fully understands the choices I made and, in fact, respects them, and that she can see for herself that she might make similar choices although at the moment she is a stay-at-home mom. I don't believe that that's going to be her choice forever.

Children can usually deal with what is understandable to them, and also they can deal with things if there are consistent limitations. It's the unknowing, and that which they don't understand, that is the most fear-producing for them. So to the extent that mothers—and fathers for that matter—can bring their children to the workplace, and let them see where they work, what they do, who they work with, that is helpful. Also, let them know that they should feel free, if the work permits it, to call you, or have some contact—paging or whatever—so they know that if there's a problem, they can get in touch with you. The other thing is for them to know that you will be home, at a regular time, and they can expect that, and they can expect your attention. Finally, they need to understand that the fact that you're away a part of the day doing something doesn't mean that you don't love them. It just means that you have other obligations.

The unknowable and the unpredictable are really what you want to try to avoid with children. If it's predictable, and if it's understandable to them, they will have good coping skills. They may not love it, but they should be able to deal with it.

Ann Getty

Philanthropist/Interior Designer

– Mother of 4 –

I think mothers working is fine. In the best situation, women take their kids to work until they're three or whatever age they enter into preschool, and then have them in the afternoon as well. Not all women can do that, and that's unfortunate. Working is a good example for your children.

People who work for me are allowed to bring their infants to work until they're ready for preschool. I think it's always important to be very attached to your little ones, so this is something I allow. I don't know how convenient it is for most employers.

Maybe a lot of us should get back to the idea of more communal raising of children and more grandparent involvement. Historically, grandparents raised children because the young mothers were too important to the gathering of food and other things. Raising the children was a grandparenting thing.

Laurel Biever

Counselor/Therapist

– Mother of 1 –

I think giving life is the easy part. I had no concept when I decided to have a child what that was going to be like. That ended up being the very easy part. Caring, that's another thing. Caring for children and being there is definitely the most important work. It means knowing that a person is dependent on you and relies on you to be guided to be happy and safe and secure. The primary goal is getting them to a point where they're going to be a good person in this world. That means being there and doing what you need to do so they can flourish.

For me there was no other option than to be at home with my daughter. I always planned on being home at least part-time. Then, after my husband died, I was the only one raising Julia. Although she has other wonderful people in her life, I am her parent, and nobody else can give her this. I felt an incredibly strong need and desire to be there and help shape her and provide that basic safety and security that she would need to be able to go out in the world and be happy and wonderful.

What is best, I think, is that a child has somebody in his or her life, a very strong figure who will be there through everything, whether it is a mother or a father. Some people don't have the capacity for patience or stamina, and if they know that about themselves, they can make sure somebody else can be in that role. I'm biased—I feel like nobody can be there for my daughter the way that I can be. It's hard for me to make that call for other people, but I know in my life there's no other person that could do it for my daughter the way that I would want it to be done.

Yasmine Ahmed McGrane

Entrepreneur

– Future mother –

Motherhood can absolutely be the most important work. If you think about it, giving birth is the truest and purest form of creativity you can have. You create something that can have profound impact on the world. This is one of the few things we can do that can have such a deep impact.

I think it's important to make a conscious choice of whether it is the right time in your life to have a child. Timing is so important, because in the first couple of years your child looks at you not so much for what you say but how you act, how you feel, how you live each day, whether you are happy. Your child will pick up on that. If you are at a good point in your life, giving birth to a child, caring for that child, setting the foundation in the early stages, absolutely is the most important work you will ever do.

In terms of the working mom versus the stay-at-home mom, I know what my personal choice would be, but I would never want to judge. If you believe in your heart that you are truly offering your child the most loving, the most supportive, the most caring environment, the safest environment, then you are doing a wonderful job as a mother. We put way too much pressure on one another on what's the right way versus the wrong way to do it. So long as you believe that you are giving your children what they need to be healthy, happy individuals, you're doing a good job. There is no absolutely right way. One can be the fullest person inside, offer the most love to the child, or not. The only right way is what is right for the individual.

In the past I've had more of a corporate career that has been really exciting. In the last year, I've taken a step off that corporate ladder and created my own business, a home and garden business. The reason I bring this up is that I think it's wonderful for mothers to think about the possibilities. When women have children, they should take time for reflection, some alone time, to really think about what their innate gifts are. Having children doesn't mean that you have to give up the intellectual side of you or the entrepreneurial side of you.

For many, I believe this is probably one of the best times in your life to become your own entrepreneur. You're already an entrepreneur of your household by being a stay-at-home mom. But if you can reflect on what your inner gifts are, you can then develop them in your own business while you are staying at home taking care of your children.

For example, with my French home and garden store, over the past year I have seen all these mothers with their strollers coming into my store, and I'm amazed every day by the gifts people have. I meet so many amazing women. One lady creates all my vintage pillows, and she started this business after she became a mother. Another lady does wonderful, artistic floor mats, and she started this after she became a mother. I think one of the biggest questions to answer as we get older is: What are my gifts? What are the things that inspire me? What are the things that I'm passionate about? If you can take the time in your busy day to rediscover those gifts, even if you've never used them before, and really understand what they are, then you can see if they become flourishing little businesses or just little passions in your life.

Motherhood can really help bring this creativity out, because we now have the time to really enjoy the little things around us with our children. That helps us get back to the core of when we were children ourselves. This is how I discovered my gift of wanting to do a French home and garden store, something that is completely different from my corporate career. To decorate, to arrange a room, and to do creative visual things is what was at the core of me. I think being a mother can really allow that creativity to come out.

One other thing is the word "just." When I ask, "What did you do today?" my friend who's writing a business plan for a company doesn't tell me, "Oh, I'm just writing a business plan," or "Oh, I'm just giving a presentation to the board at Texaco," or "I'm just writing the budget for my company." They're proud of what they're doing. Oftentimes when I ask my friends who are now mothers what they are doing today, they say, "Oh, I'm just doing laundry," or "I'm just driving my kids to their activities," or "I'm just cooking dinner." And I think "just" is such a disempowering word. As we talk about how we can raise the bar of value and satisfaction on the title of mother, I think it starts with us as a society of women who choose to become mothers. We have to empower our self. We have to give much more value to the title of mother. We can't point to our husbands or men or other businesswomen who are not giving us the feeling of value in what we do. We have to start. It starts a lot of times with our dialogue. So if we can remove the word "just" in how we describe our role, that would be one step in the right direction. We aren't *just* doing laundry, we aren't *just* cooking dinner, we aren't *just* doing the day-to-day things. These are tasks and activities that are creating the foundation for our family to live on. And it's an amazing role and an amazing choice if you choose the job of motherhood.

So I challenge all of us not to demote our self by how we talk about motherhood. We need to talk about it in terms of this valuable role that we play. In my heart I believe it's the most important work that we'll do for the rest of our lives. It's not just a job. It's a lifetime career, and it's the most important thing we can ever do.

Alexia Nye Jackson

Comedienne/Stay-at-Home Mom

– Mother of 3 –

I definitely think that giving life and caring for a child is the most important work that I will ever do. It's much bigger than that, and that event is bigger than you. You're actually living outside of yourself a lot of the time. It's overwhelming, but it is a very privileged journey, and so you treat it as such as often as you can.

In my dream world, motherhood is more clearly defined and so highly regarded that there isn't as big of a need to define yourself through "work." On the other hand, I completely recognize and understand the need for taking care of your own needs intellectually, academically, and professionally. I think there is absolutely a way for that to happen for women who are given the choice. One of my sisters does not have that choice, and that's probably a discussion in itself in terms of how our country recognizes motherhood in the workplace. So the other half of this dreamland would be that you would have that opportunity. You would have that time established in your life to be able to do other things. Then you're a more fulfilled person, and you come away from whatever it is that you're doing a better parent.

Too much of anything is not a good thing, and I think that goes right through to mothering. You have to get out and experience life and do other things. Then you can come back and teach these things to your children so that they see you being something else and learn from your example.

It's the most important job in the world. There's no doubt in my mind. Show me what you think is the most important job in the world, and I will show you the mother who raised the child that grew into that job. Our world doesn't define motherhood in this way and doesn't respect it or hold it up there. It's not really considered a job, certainly not a worthy job. It's not counted as labor in the Gross Domestic Product. There are plenty of other countries that have paid much more respect to those issues that are directly related to children. Our country has really lagged behind, and I think it's a disgrace.

Calle Anderson
Artist/Sculptor
– Mother of 2 –

I would hate to have had to choose to be a working mom or a stay-at-home mom. There is something wonderful about experiencing the stages in life with young children. I had this great benefit of going to school. I would go to school three hours a day, three days a week or something. Other than that I could be at home. I could study at night. Then, as an artist, I often had my studios at home, and I would take a break when the children came home from school and talk to them about their day and go back to work. I admire the women who continue to work and raise their children and are happy with that. For some people it's undoubtedly the best choice. But I think some compromise is the very best thing if you can do it.

I also think there's a danger in stay-at-home moms getting too noble about how much better they are and how much better their children are going to turn out than working moms. I think it's a job of every woman to make sure that she stays individually fulfilled and is not fulfilled only by her children. All of us need to feel that we're achieving something. If our total life is involved in the care of children, they become our achievement, and I think that's very dangerous for both the mothers and the children.

It isn't about working full time, but about finding meaning in life and believing in yourself and your own talent and your own individuality and expressing that in some way. I think it makes you a more viable role model for your daughter as well.

Elizabeth Colton
Philanthropist/Women's Advocate
– Mother of 2 –

We do many important things in our lives, so I don't know if I would single motherhood out as the most important. It's certainly one of the most important, because you're creating life. You're responsible for new life, and that is an awesome responsibility. It's also probably the hardest thing we do, because there are no clear answers. It's always changing. You get challenged at every step along the way. And it never ends.

Given a choice, I think the best would be if there's a mom and a dad who are equal partners—both nurturing and caring, and both with a life outside the family, but dedicated to the family so that when need be, they can switch off going to the dinners or basketball games. Then both parents are bringing something in from the outside and also dedicating themselves to the family unit.

In an equal partnership, the man respects the woman and the woman respects the man. If we can model that partnership behavior for our kids, then we could change a whole lot of society's ills by that simple act, by teaching them to grow up fully respecting each other and each other's roles. Then women in our modern communities could come to the table as partners and help find solutions to so many of our society's ills. Unfortunately, we're not there yet.

As so many of us are single parents, the key has to be that all-elusive balance. Many women have to work. They don't have a choice. So in that situation, if you can find an extended family member to help you care for your child, or a trusted caregiver that you know is loving and stimulating, you can feel comfortable about doing your job and then coming home and being as much a part of that as time away from your job allows. Hopefully we will get to a point where we are allowing our parents enough time for childcare and for going to those important basketball games and that kind of thing. So it's also a process of educating employers about how to support families, and we see more and more of that coming—again, not enough, but we're going in that direction, which is good.

I do think that most parents carry around a heavy guilt with them for most of their lives. "I didn't do it right, I wasn't there enough, I should've done that, maybe I should have done it differently." I think it's hard work for us to get rid of that guilt. We as parents are very vulnerable, and it's another layer of how to try to be happy as a parent and as an individual and be confident that you've done the best you can without carrying around that extra load of guilt, that shoulda, coulda, woulda.

Gretchen DeWitt

Public Relations

– Mother of 2 –

I think once the decision is made to have a child, then the first commitment is to love and nurture and provide education and fun to that child. The children always have to come first. If you've made that decision to have them, then some sacrifices have to be made.

That is not to say that a woman, a mother, shouldn't be maximizing her potentials. Women have as many contributions to make to the arts and medicine and education, to literature, and so on, as men do. I don't think they should give up those opportunities to make contributions and to enlarge themselves. The important thing is to make sure the child or children are getting productive, loving, exciting times and to make sure that the mother is providing some excitement and education for herself in other areas as well.

Some of us have to work and don't even have the choice, but there are so many women with talents that I would hate to think they would feel obliged to stay home twenty-four hours a day and not fulfill their own dreams. I think of my friend Ariel, this incredible mezzo-soprano with the Metropolitan Opera. What if she'd decided to stay at home all day and not sing? It would have been depriving her and thousands and thousands of people of beauty.

Tricia LaVoice

Psychologist/Stay-at-Home Mom

– Mother of 4 –

The way I look at children, they don't belong to us. Yet I am their mother, and I need to guide them. They're going to go off and be whole individuals who affect the environment and society, and it's not my right to do anything but to raise them well and to try very hard not to let my wants and needs come before the decision that I make. My father always said that children don't ask to be born, so if you're going to take that on, you have to see that one hundred percent as a responsibility—the number one responsibility before anything else in your life.

Still, I never want to talk about anyone else doing good mothering or bad mothering. To me, judging another person's mothering is the most horrific thing you can do. I think the most important thing is that a mother is happy. If the woman is happy, she's going to do really good mothering. For some women, going to work makes them happy. Some women who don't feel happy are home with their children, and maybe some needs aren't getting met because of that. What's really sad is to grow up in that family with an unhappy mother. So whatever it takes to be happy, we need to support.

For myself, I love the idea that I can stay home with the children. I will say that, as a stay-at-home mother, I've had to lose my ego. The other night we were out to dinner and a woman asked me what I do. I said, "I'm home with four kids." She said, "Oh, that's great." And then she said, "But what is your passion in life?" It was like, "What else do you do?" And I thought, how funny. If I had said I was a photographer, or if I had said I was a doctor, she would never have gone on to ask me about my passion. So being a stay-at-home mother, you definitely have to understand that you don't get some respect, as much as some people might think it's working mothers who lose respect.

Jeannie Brown

Entrepreneur

– Mother of 3 –

I think the most important work is caring for children, whether they're your children or not.

I've worked all of my life. I had my three daughters, and I worked almost every minute. If I had it to do over again, that would be the one thing in my life I would change. I would eat beans every day in order to stay home with my children until they were at least ten, eleven, twelve years old. I think those are the real bonding years. That's when your children need you most. Your children need you when they are growing up.

Stacy Friedman

Rabbi

– Mother of 2 –

Giving life and caring for children is the most important thing a person can do. It's the most important thing I've ever done. When I gave birth to both my sons, I said, if this is it, if I could just sit here and have them and raise them, this would be enough. There's a Hebrew expression—this would be enough for me. It really placed my life in a different context, just added so much holiness to it and expanded me.

As for working moms versus stay-at-home moms, I think they're both best. And that's the struggle. I think we're really looking to find ourselves, that the superwoman model of the eighties didn't fly, or it wasn't the answer to everything. We're still grappling and still looking.

I'm a working mom. Sometimes I call myself a working mom who's also a full-time stay-at-home mom because I think moms do everything.

It's something I struggle with, because motherhood and caring for my children is the most important thing to me, and yet I've chosen to work full-time. So there are definite internal struggles I have about that apart from the external struggles.

I feel particularly lucky to be able to be the kind of working mom I am, because my kids are part of my work life. They are at school right here, they come to services with me. They know what I do. They come and visit people in nursing homes with me. And I do part of what I do at home. I also feel that what I do has meaning and value, and they feel that and it rubs off on them. So for me being a mother makes me a better rabbi, and being a rabbi makes me a better mother.

Benita Potters

Entrepreneur/Community Volunteer

– Mother of 2 –

I was very blessed with being able to stay home when I needed to and work when I wanted to, because I needed an outlet. I needed something to do. I don't think there can be a generalization as to what is the best for a mother or a child. My eldest daughter is very ambitious, very talented, and she loves what she does. It would be a great crime if she stayed home with her children. It would be a great crime for them as well, I believe, because I think she needs that. My youngest daughter has always been the cookie-baking kid. If she is blessed with children, and if they can afford it, she would be much happier staying home.

I think it's very individual. There's no good or bad thing. There are women who were told they had to go out, they could have it all, they could have these wonderful professions and these terrific, solid families, and yet they weren't having it all and doing it all and being superwomen if they stayed home. That model can be destructive for someone like my youngest daughter, who probably will be happier at home with the kids, being a soccer mom. Women need to know that it's great work no matter what you choose.

Sylvia Boorstein

Author/Buddhist Teacher

– Mother of 4 –

When I die, I'm probably going to think that my children and my children's children and my relationship with my husband are the most important things I've ever done. I hope people think that the work I did was invaluable. But my relationship with my kin is the most important thing I've done. I'm pretty clear about that.

I was born during the Depression. My mother had a job, and my father didn't. He worked on a daily basis, substituting here and there for teachers who were absent at school. My mother held the family income together. I got used to a working mother. I knew where she was. I could call her if I needed her when I came home from school. I never felt bad. No other mothers on my street in Brooklyn in the 1940s worked. Everybody else had mothers who were home. I never felt bad because mine wasn't. I was well cared for. My grandmother was there. I actually thought my mother was pretty classy having a job. She got all dressed every day and went to work. I admired her.

Actually, I think she is a huge role model for me. I always expected that I would go to work, and I did. I was offered a part-time job teaching in a local college six weeks after my first child was born. So I actually have been working since the beginning. I didn't have to go to work, because my husband could have supported us. But I get nourished by going to work. I get excited about it.

I'm very proud now. I never thought of it with my children, but now I love it that my grandchildren, especially my granddaughters, come and watch me teach and see what I do. I think it's good for them.

Amy Apollo Ahumada

Boutique Manager

– Mother of 2 –

I do believe that giving life and caring about a child is the most important work that anyone could ever do. Nurturing human beings and helping them become good people is huge. I don't think there's anything to compare to it. Given a choice, my dream would be to be able to be a stay-at-home mom. I'm saddened that I don't have that choice. I wish that I had more time with my children. I need them just as much as they need me, and missing each other is really hard. I carry around a little photo album that every stranger on the planet has probably seen if they've ever met me at work, just because I need my kids with me. It breaks my heart when I'm leaving to go to work and my baby's crying, "Mommy, don't go" or "I want to go to your work with you." So, if I had the choice, I'd be a stay-at-home mom in a second to spend more time with my babies, because they are my world.

Gretchen de Baubigny

Community Volunteer/Consultant

– Mother of 2 –

*G*iving life has been vital to my life. Giving back to life in all kinds of ways is important to me, whether it's with a child or helping others or finding ways that can help cure a disease. I've been lucky enough to have all of this enrichment in my life to give back, and it enriches me as well. If I didn't have children, I wouldn't know what it was like to have children. But having children I am aware of God's blessing that I am able to have these two beautiful children and give them to the world to carry forward in the best possible ways that they can.

All moms work. There are many moms who used to work who say they work harder now that they're not "working." I applaud the professional woman who is both a mother and a successful career person, because she's keeping her brain active in those areas as well as through mothering. Where she gets the stamina is just amazing to me. I think that the young woman of today is so remarkable for the way she skillfully handles husband, children, and her professional life and comes out in a sterling way. She is the pioneer who is leading the way for her daughters and her daughters' daughters. I can learn so much from these women. They are teaching me the balance, the balance of life.

We need more communication between the career mom and the mom mom. I think you can both learn from one another. The issue is finding the time to have that exchange, because I think we long for it.

I think one of the important things, whether you're a professional woman or a stay-at-home mom, is creating traditions. When a child is an adult, she or he thinks back about home and remembers the Christmases and remembers the cookies that were made, remembers the Thanksgivings and the special time around the dinner table, and remembers Easter and the Easter egg hunts and how we used to paint eggs around the table. All those traditions help to build character and help the next generation to carry on their families and not lose it in front of the computer and the television sets.

Barbara Rosenberg

Community Volunteer/Philanthropist

– Mother of 2 –

*A*n individual has to do what she's happy doing. I know women who would be bored out of their minds with the interplay that's necessary with a child or an infant. They don't relate to that phase of growing up. They do relate to a child as it's a little older. Whatever makes a woman feel more fulfilled while she's able to share the care of raising the child in a reasonable manner will make the whole process of motherhood far more satisfying for the child as well as the mother.

If it's a necessity to work, then the woman has no choice, and there shouldn't be guilt. You do in life what you have to do. I don't think you make excuses to the child as to why you couldn't do this or couldn't do that. You do the very best you can, trying to explain it to the child. You make provisions to participate in those things that are important to the child when you're able to, and you go on from there. I think the happiness and security of the mother are very important to the happiness and security of the child.

Arlene Ackerman

School Superintendent

– Mother of 2 –

I wanted to be able to balance work with being a mom. I was never able to have a part-time job that would allow me to do both. Then I divorced my children's father, and I was the breadwinner. There was no option for me to stay at home.

I just think there's no right or wrong way. Each woman has to make that decision for herself. I didn't have a choice, so I tried to find a way to balance my work life and my children. I remember picking my children up from nursery school and taking them to my classroom with me when I was a teacher. They'd play in my room while I graded papers. I found ways to include them in my professional life so that I had time with them.

But even doing those kinds of things, it never seemed like we spent enough time together. I remember when my oldest son graduated from high school. We were about to go to the graduation ceremony, and I sat on the end of the bed and just cried and cried. My husband said, "What's wrong with you?" And I said, "I don't know where the time went. All that time that we spent together—where is it? He's about to go to college, and I can't get it back." I was just a basket case, but I had to get myself together so I could go to the ceremony.

When I talk to young people now I say, "Enjoy being with your children while they're with you, because the time will go so fast and you will pray you had it back again." Whether you're working or not, they grow up so quickly. Between growing up and leaving there are baseball games and you're rushing to soccer games, rushing to swim lessons, all those things. Before you know it eighteen years are over and they're walking out, and then it's never the same. So I always tell young people, enjoy whatever moments you have with your children, because in a few years you'll wonder how the time passed away and what happened with that time and whether you spent it wisely.

Chapter 6

The Challenges of Motherhood

The biggest challenge as a mother has been to let go, to realize that my children have their own life and they are different people. . . . To be able to let go and stand on the side and watch them stumble and fall and not pick them up because they have to learn the lesson is the most awful, awful challenge for a mother.

ISABEL ALLENDE

The challenges faced by each mother are as diverse as the ways of overcoming them. A frequent theme in this chapter is doing a delicate dance of holding on and letting go, providing safety and guidance for children while letting them make their own mistakes and discoveries. These women speak eloquently of having to share their children's pain without coming to the rescue or "fixing" things that children must work out on their own.

Challenges as diverse as dealing with illness and relating to teenagers as they assert separate identities surface as these women speak out. And then there are the everyday challenges that perhaps only mothers can truly appreciate—keeping one's balance amid the endless demands of motherhood, developing patience, overcoming fatigue, and somehow keeping a healthy sense of self in the process.

The challenges are daunting, but meeting them brings intense satisfaction. What else can compare with seeing our children grow into happy, healthy, independent individuals who put us in touch with a divine sense of purpose?

Carmel Greenwood
Author/Entrepreneur/Lecturer
– Mother of 5 –

I think a big mistake that parents make, and I made that mistake with my first two children, is overcompensating by giving them material things. It's a compensation and a substitute for love. It's a huge mistake that instead of giving love, we give them things. That's a much easier way out than being able to communicate and give love freely. That's what children want. They don't want the things. They want you as a person. They want you to show up and be present. That's why a lot of them say, "You can shove your things, we don't really want that." My two children just gave it straight back to me. They really didn't want it.

Other than that, the most important and valuable lesson I've learned as a mother is to take care of myself first. It used to be that I was always at the end of the list, after the husband, the children, the work. You are no use to anyone if you're tired and worn out and depleted. As mothers we're taught to be givers, but it's the balance of giving and receiving. To take care of our self, to keep our energies and spirits high, is the best gift we can give to the children. We can't allow ourselves to be totally run down, martyrs, in a bad mood and grumpy, because we set the theme for the whole household. So the most valuable lesson I learned was to nurture and take care of myself first and then the children.

Isabel Allende

Author

– Mother of 2 –

The biggest challenge as a mother has been to let go, to realize that my children have their own life and they are different people. I was very blessed to have them in my life for a while, but I don't own them. I can't protect them from death, neither can I protect them from life. I can't protect them from pain, from whatever is going to happen to them. They have their own destiny. To be able to let go and stand on the side and watch them stumble and fall and not pick them up because they have to learn the lesson is the most awful, awful challenge for a mother.

Virginia Harris

Spiritual Leader

– Mother of 3 –

Probably the greatest challenge of any mother is to let the children learn the lessons they need to learn without prematurely running to the rescue. I've always let them learn from their own experiences. We tend to want to help them. We want them to succeed. We don't want them to fail. We don't want them to be hurt. We want to put our heads on their little shoulders. I've had to back off on that. I've had to see that God is that father/mother of your children and that that father/mother love is with them all the time wherever they go, whatever they are doing.

I laugh, because I remember something. Our boys used to go out for a couple to three weeks to summer camp. One day when they came back from camp I'd made them French toast for breakfast. As was typical, I was cutting up their French toast and putting the syrup on it. One of the boys looked up at me and said, "Mom, who do you suppose cut my French toast for me when I was at camp?" That was a great lesson that I learned from him. Of course he cut his French toast when he was at camp. It was a wonderful lesson about letting children do for themselves and learn from those experiences.

There is also the challenge of looking after yourself. I think a woman needs not just to identify herself as a mother but to try to cultivate and understand who she is, what the reason is for her being.

A mother's life and a woman's life are like a symphony. Mothering is an important part, but not the only part. We value it as an aspect, and we want to bring the very best to it, but we need to see that there are many other components or instruments of our life.

I always say this to mothers when I'm talking with them—see your life, your day, as that symphony. While motherhood may be a large aspect of your life, like the violins are always the largest section of a symphony, there are other components, other elements of your life that bring in wonderful melodies, harmonies, rhythm, and texture, and not all of them are playing at the same time, in the very same way. If we see our life like that symphony, we'll see that there is not just balance, but harmony.

Harmony is the word that is important here. Things flow. Things move. One day may be very intense with your children, and the next day they may be away from the house for the day. There may be intense times when you're praying or wrestling through things with your children and it can be all-consuming, and then other days it's not.

That sense of a symphony helps me, and it has helped others as I've talked with them about this. If you let it, motherhood could become all-consuming. Oftentimes, those women who identify themselves only as mothers tend to live for and through their children. That often doesn't serve the very motive they are trying to express by living for those children or through them. Children, families, and communities are enhanced as mothers are like that symphony, remaining true to who they are, centered with who they are, cherishing and valuing the motherhood of their own being but at the same time growing and recognizing that they need to develop and cultivate themselves to be better mothers.

I'd like to think about my own life and cherish each day, not give away all of my oil so that my own light doesn't shine. We need to replenish our own oil at the end of each day so that we can shine tomorrow or through the darkness, the doubt, the confusion, the fear, or the anxiety of another. I say to myself, make sure I'm replenishing my own oil and not giving it all away. I will be a better mother—I will be better at everything I do—because of that.

Jennifer Morla

Entrepreneur/Designer

– Mother of 2 –

You love your children equally, but having two, you must be absolutely egalitarian with both of them. It's really interesting doing that, realizing what one child needs, and what the other child needs, and giving both exactly the same—not necessarily the same type of love, but the same amount of love, giving them what they need. It's a really interesting challenge. Children are all different, with different levels of needs. Knock on wood, I've been blessed. We haven't been confronted with illnesses or anything that would start challenging that.

Judith Epstein

Appellate Judge

– Mother of 2 –

The biggest challenge for me as a mother has been to learn to be patient, and to listen well. Those are the biggest challenges, partly because I've chosen a path that includes a very stimulating intellectual component to my career. I am used to thinking and acting at warp speed professionally. I've chosen challenging jobs that require that I assimilate a lot of information very quickly and act very decisively. That didn't transfer well to my mothering. It's quite the opposite, in fact. As a mother you have to slow down and listen to information very carefully and slowly, because it doesn't unfold at anywhere near the speed or in the logical order that you might expect or hope or require in your career. The solutions or answers to questions that you think are so readily obvious are not so to young children. They need explanations. The answers need to be modified when they don't seem to be working. So the hardest thing for me, and I think my children would say that loud and clear, was learning that the patience and certainly the listening skills needed are very different in raising children.

They are different as the children grow, as well. Communications with children can be very fragile. You can sever the lines of communication far quicker than you would ever imagine, sometimes irrevocably, and for the most unimaginable reasons. It's an interesting conundrum, given that you live with these people every day, how fragile those lines of communication can be. You have to be very respectful of that, and it's very, very difficult to transpose that sensitivity when you deal in a world, in the workplace, where communication is very quick and one expects to be given information and answers very quickly. It's just a different process entirely. So that's probably been my biggest challenge.

Laurel Biever

Counselor/Therapist

– Mother of 1 –

The biggest challenge with my daughter is individuating— knowing, learning, and believing that I need to be separate from her and that she needs to be separate from me, that we need our own things in our lives, and at the same time helping us continue to become the people that we each need to be. I get pulled back with worry or guilt that I need to be there more for her, have my whole life revolve around her, which I know isn't the case. It's hard for me to stay with my intellectual understanding of that and continue to become the person I want to become. I am who I am now, but it doesn't stop here. It's a lifelong process.

With my own mom, it's hard for me to come up and individuate against her, to not just go with what she says and believe everything that she says is right. It's hard for me to not want to follow her example, her thoughts, her beliefs. I need to have the strength and confidence to make my own way and make my own decisions and not have them made through a fear of getting out there on my own. So it's an individuation process of being strong with who I am and knowing that that is what is going to make the whole situation more healthy and happy. This challenge can be something as simple as having people in my life that my mom questions, having different priorities in my life, or it can be something more intense, like my parenting decisions. For example, I made the decision immediately when my husband, Gardner, died to keep him in our daily lives by talking about him; telling Julia that he is always with us, and remembering his birthday and significant anniversaries. Although my mom embraces some of this, she disagreed with it as well because she worried that Julia may not understand that he has died and can't be here with us, in the way a four-year-old can grasp. After contemplating what she said, I did alter some of my phrasing to Julia, such as "He is always with us in our hearts." But I held firm to my decision to do what I believe is best for me and Julia.

Calle Anderson

Artist / Sculptor

– Mother of 2 –

*H*aving stepchildren was a major challenge. I came at stepmotherhood with a sense that this would be joyous in the same way that other things had been joyous. I'd had fun and confidence with my own children, and a great deal of intuition that always seemed to work out well. I found that I was not at all prepared for the complexity of the feelings of stepchildren.

Joy is almost the wrong word to apply to a challenge like learning to parent or to be a nurturing figure to stepchildren. Creating a blended family is very complex. In the end while our families are very blended and all the children attend each other's weddings, and although we keep in touch with family news, we were a little less intense than some blended families because his children and his ex-wife were resistant. I was less authoritarian as a parent, so there was also some conflict over parenting style. I found that in the end words like respect, consideration, clear communication—words that were based upon a kind of acknowledgment that these were complicated things—were far more beneficial to me.

Early in our relationship I rented a beach house in northern California. I thought it would be neutral territory where all of the children could have fun together. It was a place where we would go together. I thought we would have these family days on Sunday where we'd make a big pot of chili and everyone would take walks on the beach. It didn't work out, mainly because of the resistance that I mentioned. Like all stepmothers it took me a lot of heartbreak to realize that I needed to hold back some of those more all-encompassing emotions and to be more discreet and also to protect myself so that I wouldn't be so hurt. In time that was successful for me.

As we went through the painful times, it seemed to me that John's children and John himself wanted very much to have one-on-one time together. We developed a system where on Saturdays he would spend the day alone with his children, and he would also see them one evening a week. So I was not so threatened by the merry-go-round of it, the unpredictability of it, and he could have this special time with them.

That's just one aspect of the way that we solved the initial confusion over how to become a new family. That was helpful for me. But the disappointments were excruciating.

Since so many of us end up getting divorced and having another life, I think it's helpful to know that the stepparent role requires special talent. It's not as intuitive as being a mother to your own children.

Elizabeth Colton

Philanthropist/Women's Advocate

– Mother of 2 –

I can identify a few big challenges with my kids, although there were also many smaller ones every day. One of the biggest ones was learning to let go at what seems to be a very sudden moment in time when we went from them begging me to take them to the movies to all of a sudden me asking them if I can go with them to the movies. I was not the least bit prepared for that, for the moment when I wasn't cool anymore and they didn't need me to go do things over the weekend. That was a big blow. That was a hard one, and I'm not sure I dealt with it very well.

Another big challenge is watching them fail and wanting to help, maybe trying to help but not really knowing how. That's a very big challenge. Sometimes, too, setting the limits and then sticking to them was difficult. Also knowing how much to give them in terms of resources without spoiling them—all of those fine lines. Those were challenging things, especially as a single mom without somebody to talk those things through with. Those were big challenges.

Tricia LaVoice

Psychologist/Stay-at-Home Mom

– Mother of 4 –

My biggest challenge as a mother is that I don't know how to put up boundaries and take my family needs first. For example, my sister lived with us for two years and she was going through an alcohol rehabilitation program. Now we have two teenagers living with us who are trying to put themselves on a good track. I have taken on a role where I will be the one to step in and help a lot. That's who I am. I love that the kids see and learn that, and we do a lot with that. We'll pack lunches and go hand them out to the homeless. We just help out a lot. The negative to that is that sometimes I don't put my priorities straight. We all have limited resources, and the more I share outside the family the less I have for inside the family.

When my sister was living with me, I was in therapy to work with the issues of having her live with me and things like that. The therapist said to me, "Why do you treat your sister like your daughter and your daughter like your sister?" It hit me in the face so hard, and I thought, "You are so right. I have this seven-year-old little girl at home who needs her mother, and I spend so much energy trying to rehabilitate my sister."

I need to stay focused on that. Probably the person who gets it the worst is my husband. Part of being a good mother is being a good wife. How wonderful it is for the children to grow up with parents who love each other! So right now the hardest thing for me is learning how to stay focused on them.

Jeannie Brown

Entrepreneur

– *Mother of 3* –

The biggest challenge with my children was getting them through the teens. That is a very different time for all parents, because they're changing. You can't believe that they're already fourteen, fifteen, sixteen years old. It's a very difficult time, and that was a real challenge to go through a lot of things with all three of my daughters. We did get through it, but believe me, it takes understanding. I remember when my daughter Carol Marie was fifteen and madly in love with someone. He broke up with her and she was heartbroken. She was alone crying in her bedroom. I rubbed her hand, pushed her hair away from her face, and proceeded to comfort her. I told her how wonderful she was and just to let him go because she would meet someone better. Teaching them important things such as respect, responsibility, unselfishness at the appropriate moments, required a tremendous amount of patience and understanding.

When children are young, up until nine or ten years old, their mother is their life. Then you go through a time during the teens when they are not your ideal. It was the same thing with my own mother. I'm not going to say I was easy. When I reached my teens, I knew everything in the world. There was nothing anyone could tell me. I thought I knew it all. My mother realized that I didn't know everything. She had the challenge of trying to make me understand that I had an awful lot to learn. When you get older you realize that your parents were trying to do everything in the world to help you, but at the time you don't realize that.

Stacy Friedman

Rabbi

– Mother of 2 –

I don't know if it's the biggest, but sleep deprivation is a big challenge. I will get over that in a couple of years.

Other challenges are letting go. My children are still little, and I find that I'm already needing to learn how to let go. For example, when my son has an idea which is different from my idea, it's a challenge knowing when to let go and allow his idea to be the idea, and knowing when I need to push mine, whether it's about brushing teeth or what to wear in the morning. He wears t-shirts and shorts when it's freezing outside, and that's something I've had to let go of. There are other things I don't. I think letting go is a very important lesson.

I've also learned through my children that to have the partnership between me and my husband be strong is really important for me as a mother—to be able to have the support of my husband and for him to have my support. My children remind me to take time and to pay attention to him and to nurture our relationship as well. I think the lesson of paying attention to my husband is very important.

Benita Potters

Entrepreneur/Community Volunteer

– Mother of 2 –

*M*y biggest challenge with being a mother was probably fatigue. I'm serious. I'm the kind of person who needs a lot of down time, and it seems even today that the telephone calls never come when I'm up and ready and willing.

Mothers get so tired. It's really a big deal, and you've got to fight it because you have to be there when they need you. It's part of what you have to do. You're just tired. You just have to get over it. Eventually you'll get a good night's sleep.

Sylvia Boorstein
Author/Buddhist Teacher
– Mother of 4 –

The biggest challenge for me is to have adult children in times of struggle in their lives and to know that they are adults and I can't do it for them. In some ways, when they are struggling, it pains me as much now that they're forty-something as it did when they were five. But I can't do anything about it. I need to let them do it on their own.

Amy Apollo Ahumada
Boutique Manager
– Mother of 2 –

The biggest challenge for me as a mother is balancing everything—balancing when to work as many hours as I do and still getting the cleaning done and the cooking done and not being too tired to have that quality time to be able to play games with my kids and not feel like, "Oh, honey, I've got to do that tomorrow because I'm just too tired." There are times when I go, "Oh, God, I've got to do another load of laundry. When does it ever stop?" Well, it never stops. I think that that's the biggest challenge—not making them feel burdened because I get tired or because I have a huge workload. It's not that I'm hiding anything from them. I just try to not let that stuff bother me and let it go. I may have just finished my work day, and I accept the fact of being tired, but I don't think it's fair that because I'm tired they don't get to have me read them a book or play a game with them. That's the biggest challenge for me, to be able to continue to do that and not get too overwhelmed.

Carol Bartz

Entrepreneur

– Mother of 1 –

The biggest challenge as a mother is the one I'm going through right now, which is that I somehow decided that my daughter and I would have this continuing perfect relationship even through the teenage years. I don't know why I thought I was so special that that would happen. So I'm disappointed as she's trying to push away and has her "evil twin moments," as I call them. I think sometimes that disappointment becomes irrational. That's a pretty darn big challenge. I don't know if there are different ones to come, but that one sure feels pretty big right now.

Beyond that, taking time for you and your world is a problem for everybody, but certainly most of all for women— not only because of children but also because of the management of the process around you. Whether it's the house, the marriage, or whatever else you're involved in, we tend to be more nurturing, and that does wreak havoc on the idea of balance. Balance can be achieved, but only over a period of time—which means that it isn't about a daily issue of being the perfect mother, the perfect career person, the perfect friend, the perfect volunteer. It's about catching these things before they hit the floor. There are periods where you focus on your children and your husband. There are periods when you focus on yourself. There are periods when your job has to be front and center if there's a big project. As long as you have a long enough time frame, your mental health will work. It might be a year. It might be a month. It might be a six-year period. But you really have to give yourself a time frame. If you wake up at the end of that time frame and say, "Oh my God, I was totally one-dimensional and I did give up something else," then it's a problem. But as long as you're giving yourself enough time, there is nothing wrong with saying you're going away for the weekend and leaving this child with somebody. The point is that you don't have to succumb to this suffocating conflict of motherhood. That is so nuts to me. Give yourself permission, or you're set for failure.

Mary Poland

Philanthropist/Stay-at-Home Mom

– Mother of 1 –

As a mother, no matter how strong or capable your child is, you never want to see them hurt. It's always in the back of your mind. I remember when Bill and I were struggling that first year of marriage, and my mother was just crying. In the car one day I said, "Mom, I'm married now. I made my own decisions. You love me, and I will always be your daughter, but I'm also other things to other people now. You've got to respect that." I said it in such a heartfelt way, and the tears came out of her eyes. It's the kind of talk everybody should have at some point with their mother or their father.

With Stratton, my son, I'm going through that issue where you separate yourself a little bit, knowing I've got to let him go on the weekends and do his own things. The letting go is difficult. Trusting them. Letting them make mistakes and pick themselves up and dust themselves off again, knowing that you've done the best you can do.

The other thing I worry about is his safety. I hear from parents how you worry about your daughters getting pregnant and you worry about your sons killing themselves. Those things are sitting in the back of people's minds. That's a mother's big cross to bear. It's our burden, but it's a joyful burden.

One thing that my mother gave me, God bless her, was that she let me go to Europe at the age of nineteen with a girlfriend. We had our Eurail pass, we had one suitcase between us. We basically packed the same kind of clothes, so we really planned it perfectly. We had the trip of a lifetime, two sorority girls nineteen years old spending two and a half months going all around Europe. I look back and think it was one of the most natural things for me to have done. But as a mother putting myself in my mom's shoes, oh my God—she was so strong, and I really respect her for letting me go. She never said to me, "I'm going to worry about you every day." She never said to be careful about being accosted. She never put fear into me. Instead she gave me all this positive reinforcement.

I remember when we were at the airport terminal and she kept stuffing twenty-dollar bills into my pocket. She was worried I wasn't going to have enough money. I thought that was so cute. But she never let me know her concerns. And that's what I've got to remember with my son.

Arlene Ackerman

School Superintendent

– Mother of 2 –

The biggest challenge for me has been the fact that you don't know if you're doing it correctly. You don't know. You have to wait for the outcome.

Motherhood is the most fulfilling role that I have. It's the hardest, too, because I didn't get any training for being a mother. I have Harvard degrees on the wall, but I didn't get any degrees in how to be a mother. It's the only job that you don't get any kind of training for. So it's trial and error. My dad and mother always used to say that you can control the process of parenting, but you can't control the outcomes. I look at my two sons now, who are loving, caring, and productive individuals, and I feel I didn't do too badly. But I'm surprised we all made it through it given the fact that it was trial and error.

Working was always hard. I was always envious of my friends who were able to stay home. The challenge for me was just making sure that I was a good mother and that they would someday grow up to say, "I'm lucky," as I can say about my own mother. And they have often said that they believe they were lucky. But it's hard.

Another major challenge is understanding the nuances around the differences between your children without either of them feeling that you love one better than the other. I always found that really hard. Both children are in the same family with the same parents but they are very different from each other. At different times they need different things. You can't always be fair. If one of them needs more, how do you respond to that without the other one feeling that you don't love him or her the same? How do you keep it equal when the situation is not always equal? That was a big challenge for me.

Donna Radu

Equity Trader/Stay-at-Home Mom

– Mother of 2 –

For me the biggest challenge was being told that my oldest son, Jameson, has leukemia. In fact, when I hear myself say that now, it kind of puts me into shock. I can't believe I'm talking about us and our life.

He was five and a half when he was diagnosed with acute lymphoblastic leukemia. It was eight months ago, and it's been devastating on many levels.

The hardest part for me is handing my son over to someone and standing there and watching them inject him with all kinds of drugs and needles. The treatment for leukemia for children is pretty intensive, and it's terrifying to watch. At the start they just blast their little bodies for about four to five weeks with chemotherapy drugs. They do it to kill all the cancer cells, but it also kills good cells. His immune system goes down to nothing, and his blood counts go down to nothing. So he's very vulnerable, and he needs blood transfusions to keep himself going. It's been extremely difficult to stand by and watch them blast his little body without being able to do anything about it.

The next big challenge for me is to keep myself in a very light and positive mode because I have a lot of fears. I have a huge fear of death for him, and it's very real to me. Just staying away from all the death thoughts is going to be a challenge. I've never been a woman who's been able to breeze through her children being sick. When they get sick, I feel it very deeply. When my son gets a fever, I hold him all night, or I stand at the bedside. Now that he has cancer, it's become more difficult because I can't control it. There's really nothing I can do about it. It's completely out of my hands. So I'm working very hard to stay with all the positive thoughts.

We just finished the first eight months of treatment, and we're going to begin the maintenance phase. The doctors feel very positive about him being able to live a normal life. So now I have to focus on letting him be himself and letting him be free and not hover over him. I have a lot of fears because he's so vulnerable. It will be a challenge not to stop life just because we have this burden, to keep all the same dreams going we had before. I have to try to let him be free and let him live his life, not worry about everything, and appreciate every day that we have.

I just want him to live longer. I want him to keep living. I go back to the fact that at first I thought he was only going to live a week, and now it's eight months. Pretty soon it'll be three years and five years and ten years. I have to keep visualizing him in the future. That's what I do. I visualize him at school, standing at the podium making a speech. I visualize him playing Little League. I visualize him falling in love and having his own children and carrying his own babies. And I'm just so happy he's alive.

I'm trusting that God's going to take care of it for us. It took me a while, but when I close my eyes and try to visualize everything, I visualize God holding him in his hands. I visualize his hands holding him as if he was a baby. That's how I have to think about it. For the first time in my life there's nothing that I can do to prevent my son from feeling any of this or going through any of this. I just have to give it to God.

There are always positives in crisis and tragedies, and I guess one of them is learning to let go and trust that God is going take care of it and guide us through it. I'm trying not to lose myself in the pain of it all and focus on the positive and all the blessings that have come from this crisis.

Probably one of the blessings is that Jameson hasn't changed a bit. His attitude is great. His little spirit is the same. He still has his spirit and his soul, and we're really thankful for that.

Another positive is that this crisis has strengthened all of our love. It's brought everybody together in our family. My husband and Jameson and Brandon and I have been here in the house, loving each other. That's what our life's been like for eight months, just hanging out and holding each other. So that's been a positive.

I'll never forget Christmas morning this year, the sounds of their voices and the excitement. I must have cried the first twenty minutes because in June I didn't know if Jameson was going to make it to Christmas. I have never experienced so much excitement and joy in him. I just appreciate every drop, every ounce.

The word is embrace. Just embrace it. I smell him all day long. I hold him all day long. I still rock him, and I close my eyes when I do it and I want to remember everything. Life is out of our hands. You never know.

Ariel Bybee

Mezzo-Soprano/Voice Teacher

– Mother of 1 –

The biggest challenge I've had is divorce, how divorce affects children. Divorce is really stinky.

Because I criticized my first husband, my daughter now criticizes him. I feel so badly about that. He wants to have a relationship with her, and she has a hard time partly because she saw the way I was with him. I was always critical of him. So she's always critical of him, and now I want it to be over. I'm very happy, and I don't have any awful feelings toward him, but she still does. It's hard for her to have a relationship with him that's on an even keel. I feel very badly about that and partly responsible for it. It's the saddest thing. The person I love the very most is my daughter, and I did this terrible thing in creating this breach in her family.

Anita Figueredo

Physician/Co-Worker of Mother Teresa

– Mother of 9 –

The challenge for me was to make sure that my working didn't impact my children poorly. I tried not to take from them. I provided everything for them that I could. I always had hired help, and I didn't believe that I should spend any time cleaning and doing things that I could pay somebody else to do, whereas my relationship with the children was something that I did. I was a cancer surgeon, and that's rarely an emergency. The treatment and so on is something you can plan. So I would plan events with the kids into my office schedule and into my surgical schedule. I attended every play, every musical, every game that anybody was involved in. That was worth much more to me than doing stuff that somebody else could do. And frequently I was the only mother there. I don't know where the others were who didn't work.

When I had my seventh child, my mother decided it was time to come out here to California from New York to help me. That added the loving relationship at home of my mother. Then I had the eighth and ninth. They just had it all, me and the grandmother who doted on them. She was a real doter. Of course, she wasn't working at that time, so she overindulged them, which they all loved.

In the 1950s we bought this particular property, and my office is right on the property. Frequently the kids would come home from school and stop into my office and say hello. And then two of them, my eighth and ninth children, were babies whom I could have in my office. I had a small crib. I brought them there, and my patients loved them. Absolutely loved them. My patients all knew me very well and were proud of my children and proud of my being who I was. It was a marvelous thing.

Chapter 7

Mothers as Mentors and Role Models

*Mothers are role models in a three-hundred-sixty-
degree manner. In every aspect of how they live
their lives they are role models for their children,
either consciously or unconsciously.*

JUDITH EPSTEIN

The focus of this chapter is the profound influence a mother has on the lives of her children. The following passages address both the deliberate and the unintended ways that mothers influence their children. Whereas a mentor is a wise and trusted adviser, a role model is a person who inspires others to emulate her. Certainly both roles are important. However, it may be that, for all our conscious efforts to guide our children, we have an even greater impact, often unknowingly, as role models. In short, as much as we implore them otherwise, children often do as we do, not as we say.

As mothers, we are the role models that young children observe the most, simply because we are usually their primary caretakers. We inspire our children by who we are and by the lives that we live. Our habits, attitudes, opinions, experiences, the ways in which we handle situations, all become entries in their guidebook. They are always watching us. It is crucial to understand that we teach behavior by our example.

The mothers in this chapter remind us that we can also take the opportunity to become mentors. This role calls for sensitivity and wisdom. As mentors we guide and encourage, rather than direct and command. Most of all, we help our children become self-confident.

The importance of our responsibility as mentors and role models cannot be overstated. Just as we need to feed our children to give them sustenance for survival, so too must we nourish their spirits in order to prepare them for their place in the world.

Carmel Greenwood

Author/Entrepreneur/Lecturer

– Mother of 5 –

A mother is the most important person in the household. She determines what's going on in that family. You can feel it when you walk into a house where the mother is contained and happy. Everything revolves around the mother, and she plants the energy in the household of how everyone's going to be. Is there permission to have fun, is there permission to say what you really feel? A lot of my children's friends come, and we all sit and have breakfast, and they all tell me stuff they wouldn't dare tell their parents. So they think I'm kind of a cool mom. They feel very free.

I think that's how you inspire your children. You inspire them by being the person you are. You don't inspire them by getting on their case. Children learn from your behavior and example. I go to the children's school and do talks on drugs. I send the teachers out, and the kids love it. They love being able to be open with you and communicate directly, knowing you're not going to sit there and judge them. That's the most important thing I've learned as a mother—not to judge our children, but to let them develop their own spirits.

Isabel Allende

Author

– Mother of 2 –

Mothers are mentors sometimes because you emulate them and sometimes because you don't. Sometimes they're mentors because you try to be different from them.

I saw my mother as a victim when I was a child. I saw her as a victim of the way our society was patriarchal. She was not educated, so she couldn't make a living properly like my uncles could. She never had any money. She could not go out. She couldn't do the things that the males in the family did. There was a double standard for everything. At four or five years old I could see that, and I started rebelling very early. Although I didn't know the word "feminist" and I didn't know what I wanted, I had the anger and I was determined not to have that kind of life. Much of what I have done in my life has been a reaction against the kind of life that my mother had. I never wanted that kind of life. I never wanted to be like her. I wanted to be a different person.

Now I'm sixty-one years old, and as I get older I see there are things about my mother that I am emulating—for example, the way I decorate my house. My mother is a very refined person. She has traveled a lot, and she has beautiful things. She's eighty-four, but she's still painting the house every year and worrying about a bouquet of flowers. She wants her table to be perfect and her food to be perfect. I realize that as I get older I'm getting to have those little things that my mother has more and more. But I try not to be like her. I go to the hairdresser, and I say, "Change my hair, I don't want to look like my mother." Although my mother's a wonderful and a beautiful woman, I just don't want to be like her. I don't want to be a lady. I never wanted to be a lady. And that's what she is.

Virginia Harris

Spiritual Leader

– Mother of 3 –

Mary Baker Eddy says mother is the strongest educator, and I think that's true. She's an educator of habits, attitudes, confidence, courage, and ways of approaching situations.

To me, mentoring is not about so much what I say or tell people, but how I live my life. Mothers inspire their children through the life that they live. A mother's life lived is what children see and feel the effects of on a moment-by-moment basis.

My mother and my grandmother were both mentors to me. They were very, very close. Every night my grandmother came out to our home for dinner, and she would take vacations with us from time to time. On weekends I would go and stay with her. I almost thought that I had two mothers. I got to hang out with them, and it was wonderful. They set a wonderful standard of morality, spirituality, community responsibilities, love, and selflessness.

After dinner I'd get to sit and visit with my grandmother. I learned so much from her in those conversations. Every night she'd say to me, "Is the world a better place tonight because of what you did today?" That was an interesting concept to get my arms around. "Is the world a better place tonight because of what you did today, honey?" Each day I knew she was going to ask me that. It made me think about my day differently. It wasn't just because I picked up trash or let somebody go before me through the door or something. It was a cultivation of the love, the forgiveness, the sharing of the toys, the joy. That is something I often think about today when I put my head on a pillow. "Is the world a better place because of what I did today?" I hope so.

Judith Epstein

Appellate Judge

– Mother of 2 –

Mothers are role models in a three-hundred-and-sixty-degree manner. In every aspect of how they live their lives they are role models for their children, either consciously or unconsciously. I think that's what women should remember about their roles as mothers.

There is a difference between being a role model and mentoring. Mentoring is probably more an affirmative aspect. One of the primary opportunities for somebody who's mentoring is to show someone what the possibilities are and how to make those possibilities happen. If you do nothing else in this life, sharing the benefit of your experience—not necessarily your wisdom, but your experience, your practical experience—with those who are coming behind you, whether it's your children or others, is one of the greatest gifts you can give. The number of choices people face is just tremendous. So if you can help focus somebody's efforts on the better choices and show them some of those choices they may not even be aware of, that is really a tremendous gift. If you don't do it for your children, my

God, who would you do it for? Help them see the possibilities, and tell them how to get there, or at least tell them a way to get started.

Sometimes it helps to talk through what the various options are, to the extent that you have the experience and can help them. Even if the decision they make isn't the right decision, it gives them a platform to move on to something else. In my own life, which I think has been a very lucky one in many respects, every choice I made led to another opportunity. There were lots of times when I doubted myself or thought I had made the wrong choice, at least in the short term, but every choice I've made so far has led to another opportunity. So at a minimum, if you make a choice and you are not happy with it, you learn that you can take that one off the table. At a maximum, it opens up a lot of other doors for you.

Ann Getty

Philanthropist/Interior Designer

– Mother of 4 –

In what ways are mothers mentors? Our children will tell you later, that's what I've found. When my oldest son started writing, he wrote a play, and he won national playwright for high school students. I wondered where he got that. He said, "But, Mom, you write." I thought, oh, yeah, I do write.

I don't know if they'd say I inspired them. I think I loved them. One looks back and thinks "I never loved them enough," but I was there. What did I do for them? I paid attention. That's love. I wanted the best for them, of course. I didn't always know what was best for them. I just tried.

Laurel Biever

Counselor/Therapist

– Mother of 1 –

My mother has had a major impact on who I am today and who I continue to be and who I want to be. My mom personifies generosity and thoughtfulness. Those are two things that are very important to me, to be generous and thoughtful, not only to our family, but to people in general. Whether it be just a kind gesture that she does to make someone feel good, or really stepping in and taking charge to help someone in trouble, she doesn't hesitate. One of my earliest memories of my mom's generosity is how she gave to her friend Rosalie's family for years following her early death. Rosalie died leaving behind a husband and four children ranging in age from preschool to junior high. I remember making birthday cakes with my mom, then taking the cake and gifts to their house for their birthdays. My mom did this without a big display to me or them. I asked her years later about this, and she said that she just wanted them to know they were special and that we cared. She also doesn't hesitate stepping in for people when they need it. On numerous occasions I have seen her get family and friends' health needs met in times of crises. She communicates the difficult things that are uncomfortable for people to hear or face in order to get the proper care for them. Seeing and acting on the needs of others is as common as seeing the sunrise in the morning for my mom. Those are qualities I believe to be beautiful, and I have so much love and respect for her with those qualities. She's demonstrated such incredible strength and determination and tenacity, and those have all been very inspiring for me. She has provided a beautiful example of being a wonderful human being.

She has been a mentor as well. She is there to talk through different phases and different things that I go through in my life. That's also what a mentor does, is to listen and help guide without necessarily putting her slant on it but helping you figure out what is best for you with her knowledge of what she's been through in her life.

Since I've been a mother, people have told me all these wonderful things about my daughter, Julia, which I eat up. Then they say, "You've done such a beautiful job with her, you can tell by the way she is." That's hard for me to accept, because she is this incredible little being with or without me. Then I step back from that and think, "Well, okay, how have I done this?" I do believe I have a part in it, and that's by just loving her and being there with her and trying to help her become who she is and who she will be without putting my judgments on her, without putting my twist on it.

I want to inspire my daughter by showing her some of the things that my mom showed me. Whatever she wants to be, whatever she wants to do, she can do it. I want her to know that no matter what she does, and what she becomes, it's perfect, and it's who she is. And that's all I want for her.

Yasmine Ahmed McGrane

Entrepreneur

– Future mother –

For me, a role model is a person who sometimes doesn't even know they're a role model. It's through their behavior, it's through their perception of life, it's through what they say and how they do it and the decisions they make. Mentors are people who I have a lot of respect for and ask advice from and build intimate relationships with. When I was growing up, my mother was more of a role model. As I'm entering my own mothering stage, she's become more of a mentor. I think when we become mothers we get so freaked out over the right way to be that we overcomplicate it. My mother never read books about mothering. She just learned how to be a mother through her own intuition. She learned from leading from her heart. She was real. She was simple. I hope to carry that on with my own children. We don't need to overcomplicate it. Just enjoy it.

My mother was a huge source of inspiration, but she had a lot to overcome. This is not a story of only my mother. So many of us might not even know what burdens our mothers have had to carry, the hurdles that they have overcome, the lives they've led. It's a huge source of inspiration if we can share those stories with each other.

The jobs I've taken, the people I've met, the places I've lived, have all been choices that are a lot from my mother. Her dream, growing up in an orphanage, of wanting to travel the world and see different cultures, wanting to live a life where you really stop to enjoy the little things around you every day—these are things I hear in my brain through stories I heard as a child from my mother. If she had never told me those stories or those dreams, I don't think I would appreciate every day as much as I do. So I just think, if you're a mother, don't be afraid to share those dreams, whether they're fulfilled or not. You never know. Your children may inspire you by actually realizing them.

Alexia Nye Jackson

Comedienne/Stay-at-Home Mom

– Mother of 3 –

*D*uring those young years at home, before you hit any kind of preschool, mothers are what you see every day, day in and day out. I don't see how they can't be your primary role model. Children know instinctively when you're happy or when you're sad or when you're holding back something, or when you're pretending or when you don't have respect for them or when you're making excuses. If you're inspired and you're happy, if you're excited about life and you tell your children that, then they are inspired.

I hope that I have inspired my children by trying to teach them and asking of them to be interested in everything. To be interested in life. To be interested in other people and to share their love. To feel like they can talk to us about anything and that nothing is a bad question, nothing is a weird thought. That you can grow and mature and become this powerful source for anything. That's how kids become inspired, because you teach them that they are accepted, that they have self-esteem, that it's all good.

Calle Anderson

Artist/Sculptor

– Mother of 2 –

*M*y mother is my primary role model, but part of it is the gift of time. I've had time to know her as a young woman and as a hassled mother and as someone who had the time to explore her own intellectual life and to share it with me.

All these different times in life it has been such a privilege to know her so well.

I would have liked more of the unconditional love that goes with mentoring. You know, "You're very good at this, let's invest in that." That kind of particularization is a very important parenting skill. In a way it's the beginning of mentoring. "I've noticed you're very good at this," or "You're so good with people, maybe you should take some courses in public speaking," or "You write poetry, let's get you into a writing program." Many of us are not good at everything, so that watchfulness that makes a child feel that he or she is gifted and special because of a particular talent is a real gift from a parent to a child. Knowing "my mother thinks I'm terrific" is a wonderful platform.

We also learn from observation a lot in families, and it's not always the thing that we're being purposefully taught. That's one way that children learn from parents and are inspired by parents. Too many parents hide their own lives from their children. Children learn a lot from times when they know you're sad and seeing how you handle it. My parents didn't really share their lives with us very much, and I did much more of that with my own children. If we were in a period where we didn't have much money, we all shared it. We'd go for a walk and get an ice cream cone and think we were very lucky. I think some of the times I've been most inspirational to my children have not been when I've been achieving or excited or joyful, although that's more my nature, but rather when I've shared with them times when I was confused or when we would talk things over together. I think we inspire children from the way we solve our problems or the way we allow them to comfort us when we're not feeling well. It's a wonderful part of loving children.

Elizabeth Colton

Philanthropist/Women's Advocate

– Mother of 2 –

I would not consider my mother a role model in most ways. She grew up in a time when women were not expected or encouraged to work, so I think part of her life challenges was that she was smart and interested in things but she had no outlet for them. She didn't really see her role in life, and that made her very frustrated. What I do take from her as a role model is her incredible generosity of spirit, her kindness. She was always very much a lady and accepting of other people as well. And she was accepting of me in my changing role as a young woman growing up. She never tried to make me fit into her model of how she was as a woman. She was always very supportive of me whether I was succeeding or failing. So that part of her personality I definitely cherished and hoped that I learned from.

There are many possibilities for mothers to be mentors. Certainly to try to pass on our values, to model behavior and how to treat others, is one of the most important things we can do. Kids learn from an early age whether you are accepting of all people, whether you treat all other people with respect. I always thought that one of the most important things I could teach my kids is that every human being deserves to be treated with dignity and respect. If they can get that, then everything else will come from it, including a discomfort with the way the world is now and a desire to change it.

I think my kids have learned from me that if you want to create change, you can go out and do it. It just takes a desire and a passion. My children have seen me live my life being very true to the things that I believe in, that I have passion for. Hopefully they have seen me do that without compromising my role as a mother. I believe they've seen me have a passion to create justice in the world and dedicate practically every waking moment in the pursuit of that passion. I don't necessarily expect them to have the same exact passions or to follow the same paths, but I hope I've inspired them to want to think big about what they can achieve and to dedicate themselves to that. Hopefully they'll find the place where they want to make a difference, and I would like to think that I have inspired them to do that.

Tricia LaVoice

Psychologist/Stay-at-Home Mom

– Mother of 4 –

I would hope that in being a mentor we would give our children something to look up to and that they see a strong, together person they want to strive to emulate. I would hope that I'm a mentor to my children in the way that they see me as someone who lives with principles and values, just in the everyday things. I wouldn't consider littering, I wouldn't talk behind someone's back. If the guy at the store gave me back too much change, I would walk back in and give it to him. If we all respected principles and values, what a great world it would be.

Benita Potters

Entrepreneur/Community Volunteer

– Mother of 2 –

For me a mentor is someone who takes the time to listen to you and to help you and to spur you on, and I think that's the definition of mother.

Sharon Cohn

Entrepreneur

– Mother of 4 –

I think the inspiration that you give your children is living by example and just being there for them every day and letting them go—letting them go to follow their passion, to follow their path, to follow their dreams. You inspire them by showing them ways that you do that yourself and that you live your life with the passion that you bring every day. Children learn from seeing their mothers go after their dreams. They can see it's possible and that it goes for them, and not to be afraid.

My mom was the one I always wanted to emulate. She's the kind of person who gets up every morning with a smile on her face, so excited to face the day. It totally amazed me that anybody could be that happy. If you start your day like that, you're going to change whoever is around you. If they're having a bad day, you're going to bring them out of that. That's what she did for us as kids.

She always found the good in people. She always helped you understand. If you were having a hard time with someone, she'd take you down their path and where they were and what they might be feeling, and she helped you understand things that you may not have looked at yourself. So she was definitely my role model.

Mothers are also mentors in every way, good or bad. My daughter just sent me a letter. She's twenty-one now, and it was an incredible letter. One of the things she said was, "After all these years of fighting it, I hope to be just like you." In some ways you think, "No, don't be like me." But she will never lose her fun, so if she picked up the good and not the bad, then she'll be okay.

Sylvia Boorstein
Author/Buddhist Teacher

– Mother of 4 –

In a certain way my mother was a primary role model when I was growing up. I imagined myself growing up to be a cheerful, gregarious mother who got dressed in the morning and went out to work and who had a good life, because that was the description of my mother.

She actually gave me many important pieces of advice. When I went off to college, she said to me, "You're going to meet a lot of new people. When you meet somebody, ask them, 'What do you do that's most important to you? What are you really interested in?' And then really listen. Be interested in it. But don't fake it. Really be interested." I think of that as being hugely a fortunate piece of information.

A mentor is a teacher, and mothers are paradigmatic teachers. They teach children how to be a person in the world, how to eat, how to stand, how to walk, how to interact with other people. I think you do it with sweetness. People don't learn anything when it's not packaged well. In a way it's like feeding somebody. You feed them information. If it's not sweet enough, they won't swallow it. Not to say that men in a teaching role couldn't be sweet, but as an archetypal thing I think of mothers feeding their children.

Amy Apollo Ahumada

Boutique Manager

– Mother of 2 –

My mom is my hero. She has blown my mind on every level.

It was very important to her to give me self-esteem. She was the youngest of five girls in a family that was extremely poor. Her mother was married to somebody who wasn't present at all. She was a single mom, and she had to work too. By the time she had my mom, she just couldn't do it anymore, and my mother was extremely neglected. She had no self-esteem. To this day she suffers from being so shy and having such low self-esteem that she can't even go to social functions where there's lots of people. It was very important to her that I would never feel that. She went without things all the time so that I could have dance classes and drama classes and feel good about myself. I remember her telling me all the time, "You're so beautiful" and "You're so loving"—just always telling me what she loved about me. I always knew that she not only loved me because I was her kid but that she really loved who I was as a person. I knew that my whole life. It really helped me feel good about who I was.

I thank her so much for that gift and for being a giving, loving person. She volunteers for the Suicide Prevention Hotline three times a week. She volunteers teaching families English as a second language. For years she worked for Hospice, taking care of cancer and AIDS patients. I mean this woman goes to the extremes to give and give and love and love and love and love. She has taught me so much about what it is to give and how much more you get from life when it's about that. She's my hero.

That's what I try to give my kids—to love life and treat people well, the way you want to be treated. I teach them to share with others. If you have anything, give it to somebody who doesn't. Life is too short to spend your time being grumpy or angry or sad or mean. I try to teach them to be good people and to have fun and to love in this life.

Gretchen de Baubigny

Community Volunteer/Consultant

– Mother of 2 –

My world revolved around my mother. My father was busy building a company, and he was generous in all the ways that he knew how to be generous, but he was very occupied with his business. My mother was such sunshine. In the morning we didn't have an alarm clock. She woke us up by playing the piano in the living room. She was a constant source of joy and inspiration and balance—her patience, her daring, her intellect in speaking three languages, her love of reading, all of these things. You know, a lot of other things can go on in your life, but when you come home and you have your family, all is right with the world. If there's havoc at home, that to me is hell on earth.

You can't be a mother without being a mentor. It's like a hand in a glove. It's fine when children are little and when they are teenagers, but it's when they get to be young adults that mentoring is much more sensitive because you want them to have their own lives and to make their own decisions. As a mentor I was right out there when they were kids, but now that they are young adults and I respect them very much, I let them go. If they need some advice, I'm there for them, but I don't find them asking me very often.

Mary Poland
Philanthropist/Stay-at-Home Mom

– Mother of 1 –

My mother taught me generosity, taught me empathy, taught me that giving felt a lot better than taking. These are the things that have served me well as an adult. She was incredibly generous. Money was never something that she talked about not having enough of. You never saw a cheap side to my mom. It was all in non-verbal ways. Always the Thanksgivings were at our house, Christmases were at our place. If I wanted a new dress or something, it was going to happen. I was never denied anything. I always felt that my mother would do everything she could for me. Being generous and giving, and getting such joy from that, means so much to me, and all that came from my mother.

She was there through all of my schooling, and if I needed help in any way she would find a way to help me. She had a flair. She worked as a buyer for a department store in Seattle, so she had a flair for fashion. In terms of mentoring just in that area, I learned that you could mix and match different things and look like a million bucks and you didn't have to go to a couture department. She had style, she had class. Those were things that were inside her. And she didn't have a selfish bone in her body. I really looked up to her.

That is mentoring. Actions speak louder than words. Children are sponges, and for a long, long time they are soaking up information. When my son is observing, he is a sponge. He watches me always thanking the people at the school or just the simple thing of thanking the crossing guard every morning or every afternoon. Then I hear the crossing guard telling me that my son is always thanking him and telling him to have a nice day.

Once I had a conference with my son's social studies teacher. He's a tough teacher, and he has my number. He knows I'm like a mother bear and that I try to do the best for my only child. So he's doing a good job of trying to wean me from my son. He just says, "You know, your son becomes his own advocate now. At this age you're not his advocate anymore." He's right on about that. Anyway, I sat down, and I thought, "Oh, God, he's going to tell me I'm a bad mother and my son's not making it." I was ready for the worst.

He said, "I'm going to tell you about your son. Your son has incredible empathy toward all the kids in his class. He has a quality in him that realizes that kids who are not so cool need someone to be nice to them and to respect them and take them into account. He thinks the cool kids are great, too, but he doesn't classify himself in any one of these groups. You can teach your child how to say thank you and all those behavioral things, but your son goes way beyond that. He does good things."

The tears just came out of my eyes. This teacher is a college professor, very tough and a little grizzly, and he was talking like I was getting a D for being a mother, and yet he was saying the nicest things. I was speechless. He said, in that stern manner, "That is your son. He's a joy to be around, he cares, and he loves to learn. He's got a very positive attitude." What a validation that was.

Arlene Ackerman
School Superintendent
– Mother of 2 –

My mother was a role model for the best that I could be as a mother and a role model for things I didn't want to continue. I remember once having an argument with her, and I was criticizing her for not being what I thought she should be. She looked at me and said, "Well, when you have children you just take everything you didn't like about me and do it better, because I'm doing the best I can." Later I understood what she meant. When I think about myself as a mother, I took the best things about her, and the things where I thought I could do a better job I tried to do a little better than she did. So she was a role model for the best things and for some of the things that I would change.

I've said the same thing to my sons. At one point one of them was mad at me about something, and I said, "When you have your children, try to do a better job." I said it with the same kind of unconditional love that my mother said it to me. It was from the heart. They will take those wonderful qualities about you that you want them to take, and the ones that are not so great you hope they'll do better.

Donna Radu
Equity Trader/Stay-at-Home Mom
– Mother of 2 –

My mother was very strong. She really did it all. She had

four of us at a very young age. She started when she was twenty and had no help, no babysitters, no housecleaners. The house seemed to always be clean, and we were always dressed nicely, and I honestly don't know how she did it.

She was so beautiful all the time. She was dominated by my father, yet she was a great mother. She still is a great mother, and she's a great friend. I've always been able to tell my mother everything. That says a lot.

As a mother I consciously and unconsciously inspire my children every day. I try to be very positive with them. I'm trying to get involved in the community now, helping others, and I get them involved. They love it. They feel so important. I did a sixty-mile cancer walk last year, and my children were so excited. They were so into it. They were at the finish line.

I think my energy is the biggest thing, and of course my love. Touching them, smiling at them, talking in a gentle voice—I always say these things are life giving. I spend a lot of time holding them and touching them. We dance together every day. Those kinds of things I think inspire them.

They're probably the most inspired by me when I'm creative. They watch me dance. They watch me sing. I can see in their eyes and on their faces how proud they are of me and how proud that I'm their mom. I think I inspire them the same way they inspire me—when I'm free and I allow them to fly free. They're most inspired by watching me fly free, expressing myself and loving it.

Ariel Bybee

Mezzo-Soprano/Voice Teacher

– Mother of 1 –

Certainly we learn all the basic things from our mothers.

We cook like our moms. We dress like our moms. We decorate like our moms. We go to the same church as our moms. We view the world like our moms. As we get older, we see the world is bigger. We look out, and we're influenced by teachers, by pastors, by other people in our lives. But I think our mothers continue to be the most important person in our lives.

We have substitute mothers, too, other women who become important to us, who are role models, who do wonderful, exciting things that inspire us. Other women have been the most important thing in my life. I've had a lot of substitute mothers who have been mentors to me. And I think I have been a mentor to my daughter. I think she would consider me one of her best friends, but also a mentor. I hope she would.

I think mothers inspire on a lot of levels at different ages. There is the time when your child is crawling and you encourage them and say, "Yes, you can walk." There is the time they're in school and you say, "Yes, you can do that math problem. You can." And then they're on the swimming team and it's "Yes, you can win that, you can swim that fifty yards." With my daughter it was playing the piano. "You can do that. You can win that competition. I have faith in you. I have confidence in you."

You create confidence in them. You create this "I can do" attitude just by encouragement and positive reinforcement, always positive reinforcement. I think a lot of mothers inadvertently create negative reinforcement, not by sheer discipline but by discouraging children from trying things.

I'd have to say that one of the greatest gifts I gave my daughter was faith. I'm a religious person, and my daughter is now just as devout in my religion. She and her husband married in the temple and are very devout. We have a very strong sense of eternity, and I know it's the greatest gift I gave her. Some children don't accept their parents' faith, and I'm very grateful that that hooked with her. I'm very happy about that. It gives you a set of values.

I've cried on my daughter's shoulders when I've been miserable, and so they've seen me at weak moments. But I've thought later, that's not bad. It's good for them to see that I have failed in some ways, because in a lot of ways they've seen me as a success. They've seen me have a successful career on a high level. But also to see that I've failed and suffered can, in a way, be inspiring to them. How we handle failure, how we get on with our lives, is important too. That can be an inspiration.

Chapter 8

What Mothers Learn from Children

*How can you not learn from your children? You
learn all over again the wonderment of life, the joy
of learning, and the beauty of innocence.*

JUDITH EPSTEIN

"Do you think mothers learn from their children?" "How
does this apply to you, and what have you learned?" These
questions open up a treasure box of wonderful insights for
us to ponder.

The women in this chapter speak eagerly and generous-
ly about the many things they learn from their children. As
mothers, we are closely bound to every nuance of our children's development. Their exuberance and spontaneity rejuvenate our spirit as we share their delight in discovering the
world around them. Our childlike wonder is reawakened as
we see the world through their innocent eyes. We learn to
"be in the moment" and to reevaluate what is truly important. Our adult defenses are no match for their directness
and honesty. If we pay attention, children can teach us a
great deal about ourselves and help transform us into better
human beings.

Carmel Greenwood

Author/Entrepreneur/Lecturer

– Mother of 5 –

My eldest daughter has dragged me through hell and back, and what I learned was that I cannot control another person. The more I tried to control and make her not take drugs, the more she went out and rebelled and took drugs and got herself in very serious situations. The moment I stopped being codependent and stopped trying to control her and said, "Well, it is your life," she stopped taking the drugs. I learned that to step out of my children's business was the biggest gift that I could ever give. It's actually my gift to let them learn from their own mistakes. As my daughter told me, I was very grandiose to think I could heal her. I might be able to heal everyone in the world, but I wasn't going to heal her. That was the rebellion. The minute I stopped, we became very close, and everything was okay.

Because I didn't go to college, I wanted my kids to have the life that I'd wanted for myself, and that wasn't their path. I learned to step aside and let them be individuals in their own right. It's a much more healthy relationship. Rather than "You will do this," it becomes "It's okay whatever you do, I love you anyway."

I realized there's no good and bad. There are only the rules people lay down to say that this is right, this is wrong.

I had friends phoning up and saying, "How's your daughter?"

"Well, she's in jail."

"Oh, you need to get her into college."

Well, she's never going to go to college. I mean it's just

lunacy. I used to get depressed by those phone calls, but now I say, "She's really fabulous, she's doing very well."

My three young kids—they're bright, bright, bright. They're going to be doing extremely well. So there's no good or bad, we just are.

Isabel Allende

Author
– Mother of 2 –

Children are our best teachers. They teach us about ourselves, about the world. Somebody said once that the most important things you will ever learn, you learn in the first three or four years of your life or in daycare or in kindergarten. You learn to share, you learn your space, you learn the most important things. I think that as a mother I learn basic things with my children. First of all I have to get out of myself. From the moment they were born I became a three-legged table, my two children and me. There was no stability, there was no anything without them. I'm attached to them forever, even to my daughter who's not here anymore. I feel the attachment very strongly, and my life is conditioned because they exist. I have learned to get out of myself, to be less egotistical and to realize that nothing is really very important. The important things are not about me. The important things are about us and about them.

I've also learned that I don't have the truth. I do the best I can, and I try to be consistent. Being consistent with the rules helped me be consistent with my own life. I realize that I cannot ask the children to do something that I am not willing to do for myself. It's not my case, but, for example, if a mother lies on the phone or drinks alcohol, she cannot tell the kid not to lie at school or not to eat sugar. You have to be consistent with the rules you are trying to impose on the child. I think that that made me more clear about myself.

Also, my children have been mirrors in which I have had to look at myself and see my weaknesses and all the things I have done wrong. They are very compassionate mirrors because they show me my stuff, but in a kind way.

Virginia Harris

Spiritual Leader

– Mother of 3 –

I love in the Bible where it says, "And a little child shall lead them." I've learned from my children, but I've also learned from all children. I've learned from the neighbors, from my children's friends, from those dear abused and neglected children.

I find that I'm always encouraging people, particularly as they get older, to have children or childlike qualities in their lives. Sometimes people who find themselves living in adult communities don't even recognize that they are missing some of those happy sounds and childlike expressions that you get from children. It's that love, that joy, that spontaneity, that playfulness. That's good fuel for all of our engines.

As I listen and watch my kids, I become more childlike. I've seen that they live in the moment. They don't worry about yesterday. They're not thinking about tomorrow. They're living in the moment, and they quickly put down a toy and run to something else. So the importance of the now and the fullness of each now moment can be learned from children.

I also learned to trust and not worry. Children trust that they will be cared for. They have such joy. They're innocent and so powerful. They make me not be so furious. It's great. It's healthy.

I had three little grandsons here with me yesterday, and one of them bumped his head. He's eighteen months old. He'd come up under the table a little bit too quickly, and he was crying and crying. Then his daddy did something, my son did something, and those tears stopped instantly and he burst into laughter. I thought, you know, he's not worried about a headache. He's not dwelling on clunking his head. He's not condemning himself. I love this spontaneity, the innocence. It brings balance into our grownup challenges and issues. I think each day we need to start with seeing the value in childlikeness and make room for that childlikeness to be present.

Jennifer Morla

Entrepreneur/Designer

– Mother of 2 –

There are many things I've learned from my children. I think one of the first things is to trust people. It's intuitive to trust people. The basic thing is that what they say is sort of truth. Their honesty is so ingrained. I think what children do is restore your faith in the human race, and the human condition.

And you absolutely stay younger, to a certain degree. You are current with whatever is happening. You have to be, or else you're out of it. So you naturally change in that way also.

Judith Epstein

Appellate Judge

– Mother of 2 –

*H*ow can you not learn from your children? You learn all over again the wonderment of life, the joy of learning, and the beauty of innocence. You relearn those things, and how precious they are, and how they are really the exclusive gifts of children, not of adults. That is probably the biggest lesson in watching little ones grow. It's a privilege to be able to see that all over again. I don't think any of us can forget the look of a child at a birthday party when the cake is brought to them. It's their cake, and they get to blow out the candles, and make a wish. You see how that simple gesture is just awe-inspiring to a child. It makes them feel omnipotent. There is no way, on such a fundamentally emotional level, to be a part of that without doing it through the eyes of children. You can talk about innocence, but you can't really know it again until you see it in your own children. That's the biggest lesson that you can learn from them.

Laurel Biever

Counselor/Therapist

– Mother of 1 –

I learn something from my child every day. The beautiful thing that I have learned and continue to relearn is the innocence and the vulnerability of a child and how beautiful that is. Innocence and vulnerability don't have to stop with childhood, I believe. Children are an amazing role model of how to really be open and to absorb and love unconditionally. Their excitement, their sadness, their happiness—all of those things are pure and beautiful and untouched by all the layers that we build up as adults. There's joy in watching kids that can help you get yourself to a point where you strip away those things that have made you sad or angry or whatever it is that you're dealing with and get back the beauty of just being with people. Kids have that.

I look in the eyes of parents, and in both mothers and fathers I've seen this awe, this gazed look of nothing being sweeter and more beautiful. I know that being around my daughter I laugh and I play and I do things, and not just for her. It takes me back to that place of being in the moment and enjoying life. She helps me do that.

Yasmine Ahmed McGrane

Entrepreneur

– Future mother –

I think we put a lot of pressure on ourselves that we have to teach our children everything, whereas it's very much a reciprocal relationship. Our children actually can teach us quite a bit. Being around babies and children, I remember that the simple things all around us, which a child sees through these innocent eyes, are more important than all the things on our to-do list. Having children can teach us about life, about what it takes to be back at your core, back at the point of just enjoying the day, enjoying the leaves falling. You can forget what it's like to be a child, and we all have that in us. Children absolutely can teach us that.

Children also can teach us about having less judgment for one another, less criticism for one another. A child doesn't look through the eyes of judgment or criticism. Children accept anybody just for the way they are. If we can remember that, we will accept ourselves a lot more as well as accept other people.

Alexia Nye Jackson

Comedienne/Stay-at-Home Mom

– Mother of 3 –

Children learn a great deal from their parents, and their parents learn right back because they revisit all the basic foundations of love and giving. Kids also teach you to compartmentalize your life, to break it down to its simplest form and to appreciate it and be thankful for the important things. It's not your couch color that matters. It really is the sky and the earth and the water and the things that are right there in front of you, and your friends, and love. Those are the basic things, you've got to start there. And then, sure, if your red couch looks good against your blue sky in your front window, it's a good thing.

Calle Anderson

Artist/Sculptor

– Mother of 2 –

Young children work so much from instinct and their hearts that it re-teaches us how important that is. Often motherhood comes after a lot of education and some work experience where we're using our heads and planning and networking and trying to manipulate life in our favor. To be re-taught spontaneity and acceptance of the whole range of human emotions, of being sad and being happy and being hurt and being delighted, is one of the most important lessons of parenthood. I remember one time when Heidi was five, she said, "Mom, why do you have love on your face?" I thought it was so cute.

Children in some ways are excuses to do the things that we would really like to do but just don't do as an adult—going to the zoos and to Disneyland, playing at the park, and listening to your children and other children. It's a window on what are the most important things in life that as adults we tend to get away from.

Elizabeth Colton

Philanthropist/Women's Advocate

– Mother of 2 –

Absolutely we learn from our children every day, or at least we should. One of the things that I've been trying to learn is patience. That's a real hard one when they're young and they're fighting over who's going to turn on the light switch every day. It's really hard to be patient through some of those stages. We learn about ourselves in how we react to various different situations and how we can try to model our own values in a relationship with our kids as well as just spouting them. Really living them is tough, so we learn by being in these new situations.

I think that the best way to learn from our kids is to learn how to listen to them without judging them so that they can feel comfortable coming to us in any situation. We need to be good listeners so that they know from experience that we will support them even if they've perhaps gone down the wrong path. To listen without judgment is a key part of that.

Children can teach us about unconditional love as

much as we can teach them. And they can teach us how we want to be ourselves in the world. Now that my daughter's getting older, I'm learning a lot from her about this new generation of girls and women and how they see themselves in the world and their feminism or lack thereof. It's a whole new level of learning about their lives and their lives as girls and women. It's fascinating.

Gretchen DeWitt

Public Relations

– Mother of 2 –

I think we learn from everything around us, and children are around us all the time. And what we learn is to never stop asking questions, to always be curious, to be patient, to take the time to answer the questions and to experience the joy of discovery. Part of the big pleasure of small children is that we discover all over again what we've taken for granted. We see through new eyes what we've stopped seeing. What I've learned from my children is, never stop having fun, never stop having the adventure. It's from being around children that one learns to be able to set new goals, to plan new adventures, to keep up studying, to think of new jobs, to keep up that never-ending quest to be someone bigger and better. Because they're still making that path. They're still making that trip. I learned from being a mother to keep going up the road, not to stop with being a mother. Just because they're still moving along doesn't mean that I stop.

The biggest thing is loyalty, to never stop loving. They've never stopped loving me, even with my flaws.

Tricia LaVoice

Psychologist/Stay-at-Home Mom

– Mother of 4 –

I learned from my children how to be humble, I learned how to love. If you believe in old souls, my daughter has an insight. I think it's because I talk to her a lot. Some people may think I talk to her a little too much, but she's got this incredible insight, so I learn from her a lot.

One thing she teaches wonderfully is how to say you're sorry. Olivia is so great in that, whenever she acts out, if I give her ten minutes she'll come back and say she's sorry and give me a hug, and we're away from it. I think the biggest thing I've learned from my kids is that it's okay to make mistakes, but we need to own up to them and apologize and move on from that. I probably say "I'm sorry" ten times a day. When I lose my patience, I always come back and apologize right away because I think that's so important. You have to take responsibility, and you have to be able to own it.

I'll continue learning from my children. My daughter is already the best little therapist, but she can call me on stuff. She said to me the other day, "How come you can be yelling and being kind of grumpy and then the phone rings and you go, 'Oh hi, how are you, yah, yah, yah.'" How many people get called on that by ten-year-olds? She calls me on my insecurities or my flaws all the time. I have to go, yep, you're right—either be grumpy to the person on the other end of the phone, or don't be grumpy to the family.

The huge word is respect. I don't know if many people respect children. Society has only recently changed from

"Children should be seen and not heard." When I'm out of line and when my husband's out of line, I allow my children to tell us. My sister lived with us for a couple of years, and she was offended by the way I allowed my daughter to talk sometimes. But I would say to her, if an adult is out of line—which happens a lot—then I'm okay with my daughter saying this isn't okay and speaking up for herself. It really comes down to respecting the child. That is one thing that I would love to see more adults do—treat children as respected humans.

Stacy Friedman

Rabbi

– Mother of 2 –

I learn everything from my children. How to pay attention, how to slow down, how to love. How to eat more chocolate during the day. How to wake up and run to the window to look at the sunrise. How to sing songs and pray before I go to sleep.

They teach me how to delight in small things. The other day my son planted a sunflower and we had it on the counter and it sprouted. In the morning the plant was dry and we watered it, and two hours later there was an inch sprout. I ran downstairs and said, "Adam, look, it's a miracle, it's a miracle, it's grown." He didn't actually care, but I did. That wouldn't have happened unless he was there. Then we went down and planted it outside. So he teaches me to delight in the small things.

And my young son—last year I took him outside, and it was raining. He put his hand out—he didn't know what it was. They teach me how to look at things as if I'm looking at them for the first time and to reenchant life. That's so powerful for me.

Benita Potters

Entrepreneur/Community Volunteer

– Mother of 2 –

I learned from my children unconditional love and what that means. I learned how important it is to be present in the moment, to be there. To have joy and excitement for someone else.

They teach us unselfishness. You don't have a choice. Why else would you stay up at eleven o'clock at night finishing a report about France and what people eat there?

Sharon Cohn

Entrepreneur

– Mother of 4 –

*O*ne of my biggest efforts was letting go of perfectionism, because I always felt that I had to get everything done before I could have fun. Sometimes this meant before I could have fun with my children. And they just wouldn't stand for that. They would say, Mom, come on, we're going to go, I need to play ball, I need you to play with me, I need you to do this or that with me. So they taught me how to let go. Especially Valerie, she's my fun one all the time. Tasha loved to hug, loved to hold. She loved those quiet, special moments, and she gave me a lot of time to do that with her. I'm so thankful. They had their priorities straight.

Sylvia Boorstein

Author/Buddhist Teacher

– Mother of 4 –

I am actually learning a lot from my adult children on how well they're parenting. I think they do it certainly as well as, and maybe better than, I did. They are much more sophisticated. I like the way they talk to their children. I like the things they say. I like the way they set limits. So I learn from them, and it's wonderful.

I teach mindfulness and loving-kindness—meditation, primarily—at Spirit Rock Meditation Center. I love having my adult children in class. They are proud of me. They bring their friends, and it's perfect. And they tease me in the sweetest ways. In my own life, I'm not always so completely wise and on top of everything. They'll tease me about that. They'll say, "Mom, I know some really good mindfulness teachers in Woodacre, maybe you could stand a little mindfulness." It's funny—they're great.

Amy Apollo Ahumada

Boutique Manager

– Mother of 2 –

I definitely think that you can learn from your children. The way they see things is through love and innocence. It's harder for me to be cynical or jaded about anything in life when I see how my children react to things. They just make me not take things so seriously. And they see everything. They get so excited over an ice cream cone. As a grownup, you are doing daily life, paying bills and putting gas in the car, paying insurance, and on and on. You forget how fun it is to color in a picture or how beautiful it is to sit down and read a book and look at pictures with your child.

They teach me all the time about patience and love and respect. I make sure that I don't fill their worlds with boundaries. I don't take them to places where everything's "No, no, no, you can't sit there," "No, you can't do this," "No, you can't do that." It helps me allow myself not to be put in boxes with lots of boundaries in my own life. It teaches me that we can be free and do whatever we want to do as long as we're good to people and don't hurt anybody and are good to each other and ourselves.

They teach me on a daily basis to laugh at everything and just have fun. They're really the sweet happy little lovers.

Gretchen de Baubigny

Community Volunteer/Consultant

– Mother of 2 –

I learn from my adult children every single day. It can be that I'm learning that I no longer see as well because they will say, "Mom it's right over here," or it can be that they have a perspective on life or a new vocabulary that's fresh and wonderful and right on. I pick up their words, and they just laugh and smile. All of a sudden I think I look like maybe I'm one of them because I talk their language.

I also learn from their professional skills. My son is quite remarkable. He has a law degree and a business degree. He's always out there learning, and he's always imagining. He's creating a new business now that is quite remarkable. As he's out in the professional world and in the world of the Internet, I listen to him. It's like going to school again. Or I can walk through a museum with my son or my daughter, and with their art history background they will teach me so much more than I ever knew about Monet or Cezanne or the modern painters.

People have said that my daughter is a wise old spirit. Oftentimes I will listen to her. She will help me sort it out, or she will see much more clearly than I do. She easily gives me advice, as does my son. Especially when it comes to relationships, we share a lot with each other and learn a lot from one another.

Barbara Rosenberg

Community Volunteer/Philanthropist

– Mother of 2 –

You learn things from your children every day. In fact, I just learned a new way to sneeze from my grandchild, which is, if you have to sneeze, don't sneeze into your hand, sneeze into your elbow. That way your hand isn't full of cold germs when you sneeze. He also told me, "When you wash your hands, recite the alphabet. That's how long it should be for you to wash your hands." So those were wonderful lessons that I learned from my grandson.

I remember an interesting lesson I learned from my younger son. We were about to do an activity, and I had planned it for his family and two children and my husband and myself. Peter, my son, reminded me that my daughter-in-law's mom would be joining us, since she's a single mom. My immediate reaction was, "Can't we ever do anything alone without including this person?" My son looked at me kind of askance, and he said, "You always brought along your mother. You always brought along Granny Annie. She was a part of our family, and Dad never said anything. So I learned that lesson from you." I said, "You're absolutely right. How foolish and selfish of me not to have realized that." That is just a minor example of the kind of thing we're willing to accept in ourselves but condemn in our children. We can't do that.

Carol Bartz

Entrepreneur

– Mother of 1 –

I think one of the first things you learn from children is their wonderful awareness of the magic of the world around them. You never go to a circus with the same eyes again. It's amazing watching children discover things and realizing how we become so jaded. I remember the first time my daughter looked up at the moon and said, "Mama, somebody took a bite out of the moon." Watching children grow up is a wonderful way to rejuvenate the spirit.

Mary Poland

Philanthropist/Stay-at-Home Mom

– Mother of 1 –

I've learned that life doesn't have to be complicated, that it can be pretty simple—and also that the most important things in life are your family, your children, the people and things that are close to you.

Kids can be so clairvoyant, and they can see the forest better a lot of times than we can. Stratton will say something to me, and I know he's right. It's like the classic saying, from out of the mouths of babes come the purest pearls of wisdom. They've got your answer. They've solved your problem for you.

We recently had a socialization issue. Stratton and a friend seemed to get into teasing matches that eventually became more physical. One day they were tussling for the umpteenth time and Stratton tripped him and the friend hurt his wrist. Stratton apologized profusely, to no avail. From then on everything was Stratton's fault. This particular friend seemed to get into trouble with other friends, too. Another mother had trouble with him and forbade her son to be around him. I wasn't sure if keeping them apart was appropriate. My son said to me, "Don't children have to learn to make their own decisions about who to hang out with?" He was right. We should allow our children to suffer their own consequences so they can learn to judge for themselves.

Certainly at the age he is now, thirteen, I'll say, "What do you think of this?" I'll bounce something off him, and he will give me an answer because he has no hidden agenda, he has no prejudices built up. He's the best consultant out there. He has nothing to gain, nothing to lose.

I can do that so incredibly well now because there's such a trust there. I can tell him secrets of my own that he will take to his grave. It's that kind of wonderful, pure relationship that everybody craves. He is one hundred percent on my side.

Arlene Ackerman

School Superintendent

– Mother of 2 –

There are times when we are the teachers, and then there are times when our children become the teachers. I've always had to be strong for my children. When I went through a difficult year—I was transitioning into a reinvention of myself from being a married person to a single person again—initially I wanted to pretend that I was still strong. They were smart enough to know I wasn't, and they were absolutely nurturing enough and loving enough to say, "It's okay. We still love you. You're still our mom, and it's okay for you to let us see this side of you. All our lives you've been the strong one, and it doesn't mean you're not strong because you're going through this bad period. Lean on us a little bit."

My sons decided that we should take a trip to Las Vegas for Thanksgiving. This was their way of helping me get through the divorce process, since we wouldn't have our traditional Thanksgiving. I have a picture of us in a nightclub and Gladys Knight was playing. I was surprised they were interested because she was part of my era. Well, they sang almost every song with me and Gladys. They asked, "Whatever happened to the Pips?" I said, "Oh, the Pips have been gone for a while now!" They said, "Oh, mom, we have fond memories of you playing Gladys Knight!" We danced and remembered all of these moments they were talking about. It was the best time, those four days reminiscing and having fun with them.

That particular time in my life was the first time that I've actually had to lean on them, and it was more about the emotional support than anything else, but they've also given me pearls of wisdom that I've listened to, and they've been right on. So I've learned to appreciate the fact that they've grown up to be become sensitive young men who care deeply and are thoughtful about life and all of the different situations that come with life.

Ariel Bybee

Mezzo-Soprano/Voice Teacher

– Mother of 1 –

I've learned so much from my daughter. I've learned from her temperament. She has a more even temperament than I do. I learned to be more disciplined because she's more disciplined than I am. I've learned from her in a lot of ways.

I always had trouble with reading when I was young. I had trouble with my eyes, so I never read very much or very well. I learned reading from spending time with my daughter when she was little because I wanted her to be a reader. I started reading children's books to her out loud. For years we had fun reading out loud to each other. Then she got to the point where reading out loud was too slow. So she'd read a book and say, "Mom, you've got to read this." Because of her motivation I was much more encouraged to read, and so now I've read a lot of books I would not have read without her, or without her recommendation or her example.

We learn things about ourselves by having the responsibility of children. We realize that we're capable of loving, we're capable of sacrificing. Probably the most important thing we learn about ourselves is that we love ourselves and like ourselves a lot better than we would have if we hadn't had children, because they bring the best out in us.

Chapter 9

The Value of All Our Mother Figures

*The qualities that significant mother figures
project are altruism and selflessness because
that's what mothers really have to have.
Otherwise it doesn't work.*

GRETCHEN DeWITT

Our mother figures are like reflecting pools in which we see the qualities we associate with motherhood and to which we aspire as mothers in our own right. The women in this chapter draw inspiration from a variety of mother figures who illustrate the most prized aspects of motherhood.

Several women cite Mother Teresa in appreciation of her compassion, selflessness, and lifelong commitment to mothering the poor and destitute. Princess Diana, too, is remembered for her altruism. Other models of motherhood range from personal acquaintances to goddesses and historical or Biblical figures. Some see God as the ultimate example of motherly care. Mother Nature appears as an example of the nurturing provider who is strong, adaptable, and capable of rebirth.

The wide range of influential mother figures will undoubtedly stimulate your own thoughts as you read and reflect upon what you value most in motherhood.

Carmel Greenwood

Author/Entrepreneur/Lecturer

– Mother of 5 –

Mother Teresa comes to mind straightaway as a mother figure because she was totally giving. Princess Diana comes to mind because she adored her boys and her heart was very big.

I think, though, that the image of giving all the time is not a good image as a mother. It has to be balanced with receiving from your children. I used to be the biggest giver, but I learned something when I wanted to write a book. I asked all my children to help me. I said I wouldn't be driving them to school every day, getting this and that, and they were absolutely wonderful. They brought me meals on trays, and they were very considerate. They said, "Mommy, we will help you write this book," and actually they enjoyed giving to. That was the beginning of my not feeling like the victim or the martyr, that I had to do this and that. I never had to do it, and that was my biggest learning—that they actually love giving to me. They'd all fight about who was going to make breakfast for mommy. That was a big eye-opener.

If everyone is trampling over us, it's because we have low self-worth. When we have high enough worth, it's a giving and a receiving, and it's a much more balanced way of being a mother. You can be a glamorous mother, you can do your own work in the world and accomplish, and your children appreciate you more.

I remember my youngest daughter was asked at school, "What do mothers do?" She stood up and said, "My mother's a stockbroker, she's a sky diver and a scuba diver instructor." They all thought she was lying. She said, "Isn't that what all mothers do?"

Isabel Allende

Author

– Mother of 2 –

There are certain goddesses—goddesses of compassion, goddesses of fertility, goddesses of love—that I see as nurturing, earthy, generous, abundant creatures, and that's how I see mothers, how mothers should be. There's an abundance in motherhood that is also in nature. It is also in some people who are very creative, who are protectors, because there is a quality in motherhood of the warrior. The mother will defend the cubs no matter what, and she will give her life for that. This heroic warrior quality that your life is less important than whatever you are defending also attracts me a lot.

Virginia Harris

Spiritual Leader

– Mother of 3 –

I have a long list of mother figures. I love the Bible, and I look to that always to guide me in my daily life. I think of Moses as a wonderful mother. We think of Moses and Abraham as patriarchs, but they had wonderful mother qualities. Moses had patience. He overcame a lot of self-doubt and fear. He had an awesome responsibility leading those children, which is a mother's job, out of bondage and into freedom. He listened to those ten commandments. I think Moses is a wonderful mother figure.

Obviously, Jesus is another—the selfless Christian qualities that he expressed, showing us that God's love is truly all that God is.

I love Ruth in the Bible. I think she was a great daughter-in-law, and as a daughter-in-law she expressed wonderful mothering qualities. I love the mother qualities of Mary Magdalene.

Mary Baker Eddy overcame so many adversities and challenges, and she went against conventional practice and wisdom to really show the motherhood and fatherhood of God.

Those are my key historical figures. Friends have also been significant mother figures to me for their qualities of grace, courage, and nurturing. But probably more important in all of those people that I look up to as mother figures is that all of them believed in something greater than themselves. They believed in a higher power. What I love about them is that they reminded me of this all the time. They reminded me when things were good and when things got tough. Whether it's the forty years in the wilderness of Moses or a bad situation at the office, or an injustice in society, there is something greater than all of us.

Laurel Biever

Counselor/Therapist

– Mother of 1 –

My mother and my sisters have been incredible mother figures for me by loving me for who I am, not judging me, and helping me find my way instead of the way they think it should be done. Just when I think there's going to be a judgment, there's not. Those are incredible qualities that my family has.

I think also of other people in my life who know when

to step in, when to be there for me, whether it be a little hug around the shoulders or really sitting down and saying, "What do we need to do to help this situation?" What they have shown me is how they can get outside of themselves and show patience and immense love that doesn't have anything behind it, only this unconditional love.

Calle Anderson

Artist/Sculptor

– Mother of 2 –

I feel that many qualities that mothers possess occur in nature. I deal with this concept a lot in my art. I have been doing a series of olive trees that are sort of abstract but are really based on these old olive trees on a farm we have. There's something about that core and that strength and that surviving and endurance and rebirth. Olive trees can be very, very old, and many of these are. Many parts have died away or are no longer producing fruit, and then another part will suddenly grow. When we first got the farm a few years ago, a lot of the trees had been taken over by the forest. The forest goes right over them. And then you see these trees come back to life. Olive trees have an extraordinary ability to survive. Dealing so much with trees in my work from the point of view of structure and armature and how they stand and how they survive gives me an image that is a metaphor for nurturing and survival, the spiritual core of life that is so much what mothering is about.

Elizabeth Colton

Philanthropist/Women's Advocate

– Mother of 2 –

The International Museum of Women has done art exhibits from women around the world, and now we are about to open an exhibit bringing together celebrations of the image of woman from around the world. The thread that runs through mothering that I see in these different cultures, from the art as well as the cultural celebrations, is just the nurturing and protecting aspect of mother, that things grow and you protect them as they grow. You see that in Mother Earth as well. Mothers from different cultures may come out in different ways, but the nurturing and protecting aspect is one that I see as a universal quality.

Gretchen DeWitt

Public Relations

– Mother of 2 –

The qualities that significant mother figures project are altruism and selflessness because that's what mothers really have to have. Otherwise it doesn't work.

I don't want to sound overly religious, but Christ was altruistic. That was his example. It was altruistic love. It was not ego, it was about the other person. That's what all of us need to do, to try to think less about ourselves from time to time and more about others. And love is so reflective. It's like a mirror, it bounces back. If we are loving, it comes back to us so we get more love.

There was a woman I met once in Hawaii who I think

of many times when I think of motherhood. I was looking for cuttings for my mother's garden on Maui, and my mother was with me. We stopped at a little cottage because it had the most beautiful garden. We asked the woman who lived there if we could get some cuttings from her, and she said yes. She took us into her cottage and gave us guava jam. We asked about her children, and she said she'd had seven. She said, "We had neighbors a mile away who were never able to have children. When I was pregnant with my seventh child, my husband said, 'We love them so much, and they've never been able to have children. Why don't we give the seventh child to them?'"

Now, this woman and her husband lived in the country, and they weren't poor. They didn't need to get rid of a child. She said, "When the baby was born, I said, 'Run and get them.'" Her husband delivered the baby and then he ran a mile and brought the couple back with blankets and a bottle, and they took the baby. She said, "I never lost that child. She knows I'm her mother, and she lives down the road. But I was able to give this gift of love to the people that I loved."

That woman is a mother I will never forget. I think of her as a mother because it was ultimately about love. When I was pregnant, I couldn't imagine handing over a baby. But she didn't feel possessive. She didn't need to feel territorial about love. That is another example for me.

Tricia LaVoice

Psychologist/Stay-at-Home Mom

– Mother of 4 –

I always had mentors, always. I love women. I have many women friends who I have really close relationships with.

There are a couple of women who I almost feel like my mother sent to me after she died.

Your mother is the one human being in the world who loves you the most. You are special to your mother. Your mother loves you unconditionally. When you lose your mother, you've lost that. My husband loves me to death. He loves me as a wife. And my children love me as much as a child can love a mother. But that's different than a mother loving you. These women who come to mind for me make me feel special. They're maternal and mother figures even though they're not much older than me. They're probably the only people in the world who truly understand.

I've shared the pain of my loss of my own mother with my girlfriends, and I can talk to them about the void and the pain. I think it's so wonderful for other women who may lose their mothers that they can still seek this relationship with other women. It does fill a void. It does feel good. It's not my mother, but they're nice relationships, and I thank God for them and what they've given to me and my children.

Jeannie Brown

Entrepreneur

– Mother of 3 –

As you go along in life and you become older, there are many, many women who come into your life and can be mother figures even though they're very young. I've had young people who have helped me and actually mothered me when I've had some tragedies in my life.

My husband was killed in an automobile accident in 1975, and I had this very young friend. She was the one who came to my house. She was the one who cooked for me. She would read pieces out of the Bible to me. My mother was not here at the time, and this young woman was like a mother. I could put her in that category of being a mother figure because she was doing what my mother would have liked to have been doing for me but was not available to do.

During your lifetime you meet many, many people who can be your mother figure. I'm seventy-six years old, and I have this little coffee shop. I have so many young people who come in and talk to me about private things. I know they do it because I'm older and I'm a mother figure. So we can have many mother figures, and we also can be a mother figure to many people.

Stacy Friedman

Rabbi

– Mother of 2 –

I can't think of anybody specific who is a mother figure to me. I think of people with general qualities or characteristics. When I see somebody stand up for something they believe in, when I see female political figures or activists, I find that so affirming because to me that's also giving birth. When you give birth to an idea or a cause and really believe in something and follow up on it, that's like raising a child. It strengthens me as a woman and as a mother when I see a woman standing up for what she believes in, whether it be in a large public way or even in small quiet ways, as many women do.

Sharon Cohn

Entrepreneur

– Mother of 4 –

Mother Teresa and Princess Diana come to mind. Their common denominator was that they just put themselves out there. They cared, and the caring, the loving, the strength to give more than they ever possibly could, always amazed me. It was very inspirational to so many people in the world. If you can have that passion in living, you're having a great life.

Sylvia Boorstein

Author/Buddhist Teacher

– Mother of 4 –

I'm thinking of the Metta Sutta in Buddhism: "Even as a mother protects with her life her child, her only child / So with a boundless heart should one cherish all living beings / Radiating kindness over the entire world." I think that's the kind of archetypal mother figure that conveys the message of how people should live in the world.

I think of the image of the Mother of Jesus, the *Pietà*, able to hold the pain of that most horrifying event in life with compassionate dignity. I think of those mothers in all the places where people are taken in the night or on street corners and disappear, who show up as the women in black and give silent public testimony to their missing children. I think they are all mentors to us about infinite pain in the hearts of mothers for the pain of the world and the response of compassion.

Gretchen de Baubigny

Community Volunteer/Consultant

– Mother of 2 –

To me it's Oprah Winfrey. Oprah is such an inspiring person to so many people. She has such empathy, and she's such a role model. I think she is exquisite and so giving. I admire her compassion, her curiosity about so many things, her inspiration to others, her giving other people opportunities, and her opening up her arms not only to the immediate audience but to the whole nation. And now to the world with what she's doing in Africa. She also has a business acumen. She is boundless and wonderful.

It is interesting—Mother Teresa and Oprah, neither of them have had children. Look at them. Isn't that beautiful, how they mother?

Barbara Rosenberg

Community Volunteer/Philanthropist

– Mother of 2 –

Golda Meir comes to mind. She was part of housing the settlers of Israel. She grew up in the Midwest, and she saw a mission and went to what was Palestine at the time and settled on a kibbutz. To me, her passion and her strength and her devotion to her cause were overwhelming. I would say that a passion would have to be a guiding principle.

Who else was there? Ruth. She was devoted to Naomi— "Whither thou goest, I will go." So many women who convert to Judaism choose Ruth as their Jewish name because of her relationship with Naomi.

Henrietta Szold is another. She was the Zionist founder of Hadassah, the Jewish women's organization, which built the big Hadassah Hospital in what became Israel. She was someone else devoted to a cause.

Mary Poland

Philanthropist/Stay-at-Home Mom

– Mother of 1 –

Mother qualities—it's something or someone spiritual, in a way. I think of God as being the ultimate in unselfishness and of sacrifice, and that to me is the ultimate in mothering.

I truly admire those people who take children who come from abused situations, or who have some severe physical deformities, and mother them. I think they're the most wonderful people in the world. I got a call on the phone about a mother who's struggling to take care of five ethnically diverse children with learning or physical disabilities. They need some help financially. I would devote tons of hours, weeks, and months fundraising to help make their lives as wonderful as I could, because that's total unselfishness. That's the ultimate—giving for those kids you know are probably always going to have to struggle through life if they've got permanent disabilities of any kind. Talk about mothering in an unselfish way. That's a gift. I have to be honest—it's not a gift I have, but I sure admire it.

Arlene Ackerman

School Superintendent

– Mother of 2 –

The people I've learned the most from about how to be a woman and how to be a mother are the people who were my mothers—whether it was my mother or my grandmothers or my aunts who didn't have children. I come from a family of very strong women, and I believe that is one of the main reasons that I am what I am today. There have been some pretty incredible men too, but the women in my family were pretty special.

I come from a line of great mother figures, not only my mother but her mother and my dad's mother. My grandmothers were women who didn't have an education, who lived in this country in a very difficult time when they were treated as second-class citizens. They cleaned other people's houses. They washed and ironed their clothes. They picked cotton. All so that their children, my parents, could go to high school and so that I and my brothers and sisters could go to college and our children could go beyond college. I think about them as women of strength, women of courage, women who persevered even when there were what appeared to be unbeatable odds against them. They were women of faith, women of God, women of love. I feel I'm standing on their shoulders, that they actually lifted me up. They said, "Just dream and anything you think you want to be, you can be." I wish they were alive to see my accomplishments because I don't feel like I've gotten to where I am on my own. I feel I've been blessed to be born in a family of incredible people and incredible women who provided me early on with a role model that encouraged me to be anything.

So when I think about women I admire, whether they're mothers or not, I'm looking for strength. I'm looking for courage. I'm looking for women who are spirit-filled and godly. I'm looking for women who know how to love and who love life.

Ariel Bybee

Mezzo-Soprano/Voice Teacher

– Mother of 1 –

I have some of my very own personal mother figures, women who have been important and influential in my life and who have taken me on and done things for me that my own mother couldn't do. They are women I met partly because I was a singer and I was fairly prominent. Women took me under their wing and encouraged me and set great examples for me about accomplishing and what I could do. That's been extremely important to me. Unfortunately, my mother's example to me was "I can't do." You know, "I can't do everything." "I can't put up with this tough life." Other women have proved the opposite to me, that you can do whatever you want and you can probably have it all. Yes, I have very accomplished women who were great examples to me.

Anita Figueredo

Physician/Co-Worker of Mother Teresa

– Mother of 9 –

*O*h, what a force in my life Mother Teresa was. She was a close friend for forty years.

I read the first article about her that was published in the United States. I was very touched by the description of what she was doing. She was picking dying people up off the streets in Calcutta and nursing them, not necessarily back to health. Practically nobody survived. But she had a home for the destitute dying, and she loved them. She gave them the only love they'd ever had. The example as described in the article was something that you had to admire.

It affected me enough that I wrote her a letter. I told her that I too worked with the dying and the very ill, but that I did it under the most comfortable conditions, with all kinds of assistance, a good location, and everything else. I could do everything for them. I told her that I was a frustrated missionary and that she was doing the dirty work, and how much I appreciated what she was doing.

At that time, 1958, not only was there no fax and no e-mail or anything else, but I really think that correspondence to India went by dolphin. So weeks later, to my amazement, I received a letter in her handwriting telling me that she had read my letter to the assembled nuns and that she prayed we would meet. And I now know from experience that when Mother Teresa prays for something, it happens. Don't count it out.

We had this very desultory correspondence, because it took so long for letters to go back and forth. Then in 1960 she wrote saying that she was coming to the United States for the first time and that she prayed that we would meet. There it was again. I remember saying to my husband, "You know what, honey? She's probably coming to New York, and she thinks that because that's the United States, we'll meet." I had forgotten that before she founded the Missionaries of Charity she was a teacher, and she was a teacher of geography. She knew exactly where New York was and where California was.

Sometime after that I came home from work, and the morning paper was still on the dining room table, and there was a picture of Mother Teresa. The paper said she was speaking that night in San Diego. Well, I had to meet her. There was no question about it. So I called a friend and talked her into going with me, and we drove down to the place.

After her talk we got to meet her, and I said, "Mother Teresa, I'm Doctor Figueredo." And she said, "Anita, I prayed that we would meet." Then she embraced me and walked off with me. She left the people who were still there to meet her.

When I came home, I said to my husband, "I have been touched by the hand of God. I've been about two feet off the ground." It was the most remarkable thing that's ever happened to me.

After that I became very aware of her and everything she did. Our relationship only deepened.

In 1964 Bill and I took a trip around the world with a medical group. We picked a route that would take us to Calcutta, so I went to visit her. That was a marvelous experience. She took us to every one of her places, the home for the destitute and dying, the disabled children's place that she had. We saw everything she dedicated herself to.

Years later, in 1972, Bill and I were going to the Middle East. The Pontifical Mission for Palestine had asked us to do a survey of the medical facilities that were available to Palestinian refugees in their camps. We went first to Beirut, Lebanon. When we got there, our escort said that he had to stay at the airport and pick up a nun coming in from India. I said, "Mother Teresa?" And he said, "You know her?" I said, "Yes, I know her."

So we waited. Sure enough, Mother Teresa came. It was her first visit to the Middle East, and it coincided with ours.

She didn't have any idea that we were coming. When we met, she said, "Anita, what do you suppose God wants us to do together here?" Oh, by golly, He had a few plans.

She was going to Jordan. We went on with our visit to the refugee camps that were in that general area, and then went on to Jordan, which had been our plan. When we got there and saw Mother, she said, "Oh, Anita, you came. I need you now. We're going to the only place they have for the sick refugees. It is in the Jordanian desert. We can't have that. They have to be where the people are so that the people can help them." That was always a concept of hers. The sick weren't to be hidden away. They were to be brought out.

So we spent the next ten days negotiating with some of the local Jordanian people and arranging for a place in Amman where these people could be taken care of. I found myself negotiating with Mother. She did all the smart negotiating. All I had to do was shake my head yes and at least lend a little weight to the proposal and so on.

After that she was coming to New York. Sure enough, we were going to New York also. That was part of our trip. When we met in New York, she said, "Anita, are you a co-worker?" I'd never heard the term before except in general language. I said, "Sure, Mother." And she said, "Well, there's just been founded the Co-workers of Mother Teresa in America, and we're having the first meeting this week." I was not able to attend the meeting, but when I got home I had a visit from a priest from Los Angeles who had attended it. He was one of the first Co-workers of Mother Teresa. He said, "Doctor, Mother Teresa would like you to take charge of the Southwestern United States." Just a little thing. Well, compared to India, it was. I mean, nothing was too big. So I became the link for the Co-workers of Mother Teresa in the Southwestern United States.

Being a member of that group was remarkable because for a period of several years we met with Mother every year for a full weekend. During that weekend, we saw her all the time. She was with us. She listened to what we had to say. She told us her own stuff. Knowing her, working with her, was one of the great things in my life for sure. Imagine.

I went to her beatification, yes. If you can believe it, I was one of ten people in the world who were selected to receive Communion from the pope. I have been truly blessed. If I ever had a complaint I'd have to have my head examined.

So what do I think of, when I think of Mother Teresa? Well, her utter sincerity. There was never a devious anything in her mind. And she taught me all about loving people unconditionally. She just loved everyone. I remember she would say, when we were having those meetings with her, "Don't just love the poor and the needy. Look across the table from you and see who in your family needs your love." She'd make a point of those things, and you couldn't forget them.

Chapter 10

A Mother's Friendship

*I think a mother is the best friend that God gives
us. There are friend moments, and there are
mother moments. Sometimes they are both
at the same time.*

VIRGINIA HARRIS

"Is it difficult to be both a friend and a mother to your children?" "How do you think this can be achieved?"

The concept of a motherly friendship *seems* straightforward. Certainly affection, concern, and support are common to both mothering and friendship. Given the depths of a mother's love and the intimate knowledge she has of her child, what better friend could a child wish for? Yet many women in this chapter struggle with the complexities of this issue. While a friend may listen and offer uncritical support, a mother's special responsibility for the welfare of her child often takes precedence over a friend's response. A mother is not a peer; she is a source of guidance and direction. How then do we draw the line between mother and friend so that we do not confuse our children?

Some of the women in this chapter find it difficult to establish these boundaries, while others see little conflict. Several point out that the mother-child relationship evolves as the child matures and that it is easier and more rewarding to be friends when the child becomes an adult. But wherever we may draw the line, friendship and motherhood share a mutual trust and respect. We need to listen to our children and respect their individuality through each stage of our relationship with them.

Perhaps the single thread that ties together the myriad points of view offered in this chapter is the uniqueness of the mother-child relationship. A child will have many friends in life, but only one mother.

Carmel Greenwood

Author/Entrepreneur/Lecturer

– Mother of 5 –

How can you be both a mother and a friend to your children? By being totally honest and communicating with them.

A mother also has to have the discipline. A friend would just listen to your problem, but children are coming to you as a mother for advice. I think it's a mother's role not to let them get away with any bullshit. I call them on what they're doing and tell them that I can see through their patterns. But I've learned that. I let my first two get away with murder, and I was a real soft touch. Now I'm really strong. Nobody gets away with anything. I've come from being the martyr and doormat because I desperately needed to be needed and loved, but now I don't have that need. I get a lot of respect. I have a much more firm ground and a better grip on being a mother.

The biggest thing I learned was to say no. I learned that only much later on. I actually wrote it on my hand. I remember when I first started saying no to my eldest daughter. She couldn't believe it. She was kicking doors in and having real temper tantrums because I never, ever said no. Now it's my favorite word. I love it so much. And it works.

Isabel Allende

Author

– Mother of 2 –

I've been a friend and a mother to my children. I don't think it's difficult. I have been very clear about the fact that I'm a mother, and as a mother I have certain responsibilities, certain obligations, and certain rights that friends don't. I have been friendly in the sense that I have been there with my kids in every moment of their life and we can talk about everything. We talk about money, about sex, everything. We're real friends.

I think this can be achieved if from the very beginning you realize that they are different people and you treat them with respect. The fact that they are young, that they are little, that they are dependent doesn't make you the powerful figure. They are powerful too. I always had great respect for them, and I demand equal respect. So in my house it was totally impossible and unacceptable that a child would yell back at you, because you didn't yell at them. There was no slamming of doors and no insulting. There was consistency and respect.

Virginia Harris

Spiritual Leader

– Mother of 3 –

I think a mother is the best friend that God gives us. There are friend moments, and there are mother moments. Sometimes they are both at the same time.

I have appreciated being both a mother and being a friend, and I've never seen it as difficult. I think I have achieved that by listening to them and by being flexible, being humble, and setting aside my own preconceived ideas of how they should do something. To be a friend and a mother, you can't go into a conversation about something thinking that you know what the answer is or where this conversation should come out. You need to respect your children as unique individuals, not treat them as little people with less knowledge. Respect their ability to know and come forward with intelligent answers and actions. Sometimes they are very simple, but they are the right ones. Respect the way they are going to work things through. Let them learn as they go. Enjoy learning with them, and enjoy having them come as that friend and tell you about them.

It's a little bit like when we teach children to learn how to ride a bicycle. We don't get on the bicycle and ride it for them. There are training wheels. They have to sit in the seat and take the handlebars in their own hands. We go beside them, and that builds up their confidence. The day we take the training wheels off, we usually run beside them so they don't fall over. That's when you're being a friend, when you run beside them.

Friendship comes from all those days you spend listening to them talk to you. My boys are thirty and thirty-two and thirty-five, and when they come to visit we have wonderful talks. They are great communicators. They are great listeners. They give me great guidance. I love that.

My daughter-in-law paid me a huge compliment at Christmastime. She has a relationship with her mother, but she said, "With you it's different. You're my best friend." She said, "I never feel like my mother allows me to be a friend. She always wants to be my mother. What I love about you is that you're both my mom and my best friend." Coming from a daughter-in-law, that's pretty awesome.

Judith Epstein
– Mother of 2 –

I think there's a distinction to be made between your roles as a mother of young children versus adult children. I'm of the school that it's really difficult to be a friend to your children when they're young, and I think it's confusing. They have lots of friends, and I think it's important that they grow through the unique relationship of your being their mother because the roles are very different, especially for a young child. This goes back to that fine balance about being the source of unconditional love and yet also being the source of wisdom or of how to make their way in the world, which involves some yeses and some nos, some permission and some not.

There's a Latin expression: *Multa corda, una causa.* Many hearts, one purpose. There can be many friends, but one mother. Children need to know that, because friends may desert them, or friends may support them in times when they shouldn't be supported. Friends play a different role. Friends may be there to amuse them, and friends may be there to listen to their inner thoughts as well. A mother's role is unique, and I think it's confusing to try to and be more than one role for a child. It prevents you from being consistent, which is so important.

Having said that, one of the greatest joys of having adult children is to be their friends and to enjoy that new relationship. So how does that happen? At some point, we all have to let our children go, painful as it might be, and as wrenching as it is to the mothering instinct in us. But at some point they need to be stand-alone adults. When you're confident that that separation has occurred, it is a great joy and delight to approach them with a new relationship as a friend. That you do by sharing experiences and interests, whether it's taking vacations together, going to the symphony together, shopping together, or cooking together. It's shared activities, like you would have with other friends, and interests that are independent of the family relationship. Of course, the relationship is always infused with the original parenting relationship, because that's never going to go away. But that's why you can be friends with adult children, even though it's not a good idea when your children are small.

Ann Getty

Philanthropist/Interior Designer

– Mother of 4 –

You have to wait. I don't think that you're a friend to a young boy. You're a mother, and that's what they want. I did not want to have heart-to-heart discussions with a fifteen-year-old about girls, and sex, and the locker room talk. I suppose if I'd had daughters, I would have wanted this kind of intimacy, which I would still consider not friendship, but mothering.

I don't know how you separate it. Of course you're a friend, and you're a mother, and you're there. But primarily you're a mother. My boys wouldn't be my first choice for buddies. And they would find it embarrassing for me to be a buddy.

Laurel Biever

Counselor/Therapist

– Mother of 1 –

A mother's connection is just a deeper kind of friendship. It's not always fun to teach and guide instead of just being there to listen and have fun. There is a balance, because you can't want only to please your children. I want my daughter to be happy all the time. I want her to be safe all the time. I also want her to know that that's not the real world, and I need to be there to help her struggle through it and not just try to fix it. I need to let her know that she has me as a strong, stabilizing force in her life and that we'll get through whatever needs to be gotten through.

It's not about making things okay. It's about being there. Making things okay would be such a disservice, because growth comes from struggle. Growth comes from both pain and happiness. Look at my situation with losing my husband. It was the most horrible experience I've ever gone through, and it was the most beautiful experience I'd ever gone through. To be able to be there for him in an unconditional way and learn from him, from his graciousness and his beauty, and how he struggled, and how he allowed me to be there with him. He taught me so much about that, and I am a much better person for it. I can be there for Julia in so many other ways because of that experience. I understand that things aren't going to be easy and that life can be hard and really painful, and yet there are beautiful things that can come out of that.

Yasmine Ahmed McGrane

Entrepreneur

– Future mother –

You can be a friend and a mother to your child, but the number one thing children need first is a mother. There is a core difference between being a mother and being a friend. I have a lot of friends who I go to for advice, but I have only one mother. I respect my mother in a different way than I respect a friend in the sense that my mother has taught me the core things of who I am and what life is. She has also taught me how to set boundaries. It's really important to teach your child when they leave the nest how to take those boundaries and make good choices. If you're too much of a friend to your child, sometimes you put too much hardship on your child to have to make those parental decisions. When children leave the nest, they need to feel very confident inside that they know how to deal with whatever comes their way—loss, hardship, heartache. They can make those decisions a lot better if you first play the role of mother versus playing the role of friend.

I see a lot of adolescents and even children who are almost playing the role of parent with their mother and father. I think it's because a lot of parents are afraid that their children won't love them. Remember that your child will always love you first and loves you a lot more than you probably realize. But your children will love you more if you give them what they need to be successful in life.

Alexia Nye Jackson

Comedienne/Stay-at-Home Mom

– Mother of 3 –

The first and primary role has to be as mother and as a person who has given structure to life. Children have to know the boundaries, and you have to be able to show them that first. That's the greatest love, and they know that.

You have to be a foe sometimes to be a friend. You listen to maternal instinct and intuition, and if you're really loving your children and you're paying attention to them, you know that it's structure and it's balance and it's direction you give your kids first. As they mature and leave this environment and have been given the tools to go out and deal with the world, you hope that they come back and that the words they say are "Thank you," because they know it.

I think your kids want friendship from you. They want to know that you're a friend. They look at you as a person who loves them and adores them and laughs with them and cuddles with them and takes them places, who sacrifices for them and is there for them. Just when they turn to you to be a friend and hope that they can stay out until two o'clock at this fun party, you're not there. That's almost a line of deceit or something in the mind of a young human being. In fact friendship happens right along the lines of loving discipline because they're just not mature enough. One of your jobs is to know where the line is. So they're not confused, tell them outright, "I have to be a parent first. I think you're going to turn out to be a great friend of mine, and I love watching you do things. But let's face it, the things you do with your friends are not really things you do with me. We're friends of another kind, and it's a good thing."

Elizabeth Colton

Philanthropist/Women's Advocate

– Mother of 2 –

I'm not sure that I have achieved being both a mother and a friend, but I think trying to be a friend is about being open, listening without judgment. That's the most important thing you can do as their friend, and then if they trust that you're not going to judge them, they'll be more open to listening to whatever kind of guidance you might be able to give them from your own experiences. So to be able to keep the limits that you need to set as a parent, but also help them make their decisions within those limits, would be a good goal.

It also makes a big difference if along the way you can find activities that you enjoy sharing together, be it shopping or baking or listening to music or traveling or skiing or whatever—common ground. We take one trip together every summer, and that's really a nice venue for reacquainting myself with my kids and exploring, discovering the world together.

Gretchen DeWitt

Public Relations

– Mother of 2 –

*I*t's difficult to be a friend and mother sometimes because the child can perceive the mother or parent as a peer, and we are not their peers. We are their mentors, their providers. We're older, we're wiser, and it doesn't really work for them to treat us as peers all the time. There has to be some recognition that respect has to be put into play and that there are rules that have to be abided by because they're put in place for the safety of the child.

There were times maybe when I did treat my children as if they were my buddies. They were my friends, and they are my best friends. But I think sometimes they go into a gray area where the authority is diminished because we've maybe been buddies too much. Children need to understand that parents have the right and obligation to make life safer, and making life safer means that there are rules.

I think you achieve this through communication, by saying "You're my best friend, but I'm responsible for you. It's my responsibility to safeguard your health and well-being and happiness, and in order to do that I have to be the one making some of the important decisions until you're old enough to make these decisions for yourself." And I think that has to be drawn in cement very early so there's no equivocating later on. You have to make them understand that this is about love, it's not about control. It's not about who's the boss. It's about the fact that my role is to protect you from unhappiness and harm. Because I love you, I'm going to need to take care of you the best way I can.

Tricia LaVoice

Psychologist/Stay-at-Home Mom

– Mother of 4 –

I believe so much that my children have to be able to talk to me, and I also live by the motto that I will teach nothing to my teenagers. So whatever I want instilled in them, I will do it now, before they get to the point where they will not be hearing me so much. I try hard to be their friend. I try to lay in bed quietly with each one of them every night and rub their back in the silence and peace and safety of their room, listening to what they have to say. I want to create that base now so that when they become a little bit older they still see me not just as a parent but as a parent and friend, as someone they can trust.

It's hard sometimes to balance those roles. Yesterday my daughter got in the car and said, "Oh, my artwork stinks, and everybody else's is great." I wanted to say, "Olivia, come on, your artwork is beautiful." It was back to being the parent. It's really hard for me to sit back more as a friend and listen. You want to fix it. But sometimes they just want you to listen, and that's being a friend. I could have tried to fix it, and I wanted to, but I thought, "You know what, it's okay that this is tough for her right now, and I'm going to listen to her because that's what a friend would do."

Jeannie Brown

Entrepreneur

– Mother of 3 –

I am seventy-six, and the most wonderful thing in the world is that my three daughters and my granddaughter are my friends. My children respect me as the mother, they listen to me, but at the same time we are very, very close friends. My children really treat me like a friend. We go out to lunches and we're friends. We go shopping. We go out just to buy lipsticks. We go out to buy earrings. We love to giggle and laugh, and we have fun together, and, yes, we're friends. At the same time I'm the mother, and they treat me with much love.

I am a mother, but at the same time I know that I am my children's best friend. I think it develops over many years. It is not an overnight thing. It's what happens in a full life. I've lived a full life, so I'm at the point where I'm receiving all of this at this late age, which is when mothers do receive it. Your children have lots of friends when they're young, and they talk to them and tell them things they don't tell their mother. But as time passes on and you get older, the feeling that you get to have with your children is absolutely wonderful.

I tell my daughters that the most important thing that I've learned is to build a life and have beautiful, beautiful memories. I remember holding hands with my mother in a movie. I'm seventy-six years old, and I've remembered that all my life. So build memories. Do things that are wonderful. Never do things that are going to really hurt. Don't say things that hurt your children. Build good memories.

Benita Potters

Entrepreneur/Community Volunteer

– Mother of 2 –

*F*riendliness is certainly part of being a mother. You want to be able to have those friendship conversations, and the lines are not always so cut and dried. You can giggle with them at a coffee shop just like a friend, or talk about an email that a boyfriend has written. It's certainly more of a friend activity than a mother activity. But even so, being a mother comes first, and that should be in the forefront of your mind. It is the most important relationship. Friendship is kind of incidental. They will only have one mother. They will have a lot of friends.

Sharon Cohn

Entrepreneur

– Mother of 4 –

I think we're friends with our kids until they're about twelve years old, somewhere in there. They are so much fun to be with. I can't explain what fun I had with my kids up to that point, and then it was work. There were a lot of moments in that work that were wonderful as well, but it definitely changes, and the friendship is harder. You have to keep being there and letting them always know that you're going to be there for them if they need you, no matter how they fight you silently or at the top of their lungs. I think that's what they want to know and why you go through that difficult time. It's so they get that feeling engraved that you will be there no matter what. Then you finally get there, and it's time for them to go. And then it's okay because you both know that you're going to be there for each other.

Sylvia Boorstein

Author/Buddhist Teacher

– Mother of 4 –

Especially as my children are older, it's easier to be friends with them. We all have the same kind of struggles as grownups, and we care about each other, so we're friends. I have a very close relationship with all my children. They're friends with each other, and they're friends with me. I think you can draw the line without being an adversary.

Amy Apollo Ahumada

Boutique Manager

– Mother of 2 –

I couldn't imagine not being friends with my kids. I thoroughly enjoy them and have a good time with them just as I would with my friends. But you need to be a mother first. Yes, you would hope your kids like you. But I think there was a huge misconception in the seventies when all these moms were told to be friends and not mothers. So they thought, "Well, if I'm a friend with my kid, then I'm cool and my kid will really love me." Then, when the kids really needed them to be the mother, they weren't there.

I think there's a huge difference in how your kids will relate to you if you are both a mother and a friend. Being their friend means taking the time to know them, to love and respect them for who they are, and getting to know what they like and dislike, as you would a friend. Then when as a mother you're telling them, "No, don't do this," they're much more open to listen to why rather than to think, "Oh, God, that's just my mom saying no again because she's Mom."

My mother's my best friend. And she's still my mother. I could not see her differently. Even friends set boundaries with each other, and that's to keep each other safe.

Gretchen de Baubigny
Community Volunteer/Consultant

– Mother of 2 –

I was on the alert about that transition from being a mother to being a friend, and yet I don't know how much of a transition it really was except for my letting go a little bit more. I think we've always been friends. It can be just talking in the car when they're young—"Oh, Johnny did this, and so-and-so has a new pair of dancing shoes." Talking about things at their level and being at their level is friendship and not just being mom. Now that they are young adults, I think our relationship is one of more friendship. In friendship we share our experiences, and everything is respected. You're never criticized for making too much out of this or too much out of that. We respect one another, and we listen. The gift of listening and responding is important.

Barbara Rosenberg
Community Volunteer/Philanthropist
– Mother of 2 –

I don't think you can be a friend to your kids when they are young. When you say, "Don't cross the street," it means "Don't cross the street or there's going to be dire consequences. Do not do it." There has to be a great sense of being absolute in the children's youth. If you're lucky and you respect your children and enjoy your children in adulthood, then you can be a friend if they'll have you as a friend or you want them as a friend. But again I think respect is a vital part of that relationship.

Mary Poland
Philanthropist/Stay-at-Home Mom
– Mother of 1 –

You've got to relate to your children at different ages and try to empathize with that level of maturity and emotionalism and talk to them as a friend. But you are a mother first. You are a friend second. I've seen cases, even in my own family, where a mother is more a friend, putting the friendship first and the mothering second. I don't think the children had all the boundaries that they should have, nor was the bar always raised as high as it could have been raised. It was more like "Let's be friends and giggle and laugh." Because of that there were conflicting messages. Then you don't know what being a mother really is. It gets a little confusing for the child or the young adult.

What I'm going to be adamant about is, be a mom first. Yes, you're a friend, a confidant, someone who a child can give their deepest, darkest secrets to, and it'll go to your grave. But you are a mom first. I don't think there's a kid in the world who doesn't want that. They may not know it in the instant when they are kicking and screaming, but they know subconsciously. They hold that inside, that that was the hardest thing for you to do. That's what they want. That's what they grab on to and carry with them the rest of their life, that their mom said things to them to teach them.

Donna Radu

Equity Trader/Stay-at-Home Mom

– Mother of 2 –

Before I had children I always said you couldn't be both a friend and a mother, but of course you can. My mother did a great job of it on a certain level. I could tell her just about anything. There were a lot of things I didn't tell her, but I think that's because she never really opened up a lot of lines of communication. She didn't initiate conversations about life phases, about things that were coming up in my life or that I might confront. But anything I was going through, she was there for.

Now I tell my mother everything. She loves to hear what goes on in my life and wants to talk every day, and it doesn't go anywhere else. She always seems to say the right things—not giving a lot of advice, but just listening to me.

Because I finally let her listen to me, I think it's so important with my boys. They're only five and a half and three. They're not afraid to talk to me and tell me things, and I want them to go through the rest of their life being that way. I plan on making sure that I'm always going to create an environment where they can pull their chair up and talk to me and not have any fears or anxiety about what I might say or do. But I do think there are boundaries, and I have to draw lines. It's very important for children to know where your boundaries are as a mother, but at the same time to be able to share a unique friendship. A sense of respect is really important to give to your children. I give my boys a lot of respect. Learning how to talk to them is key. It's important to use the right words when you're talking to your children. So often, if you use the wrong words, children shut down and stop listening, because all they can do then is feel. They don't hear anything.

Another part of it is one-on-one time, making time for each other and experiencing each other as individuals. And finally, you have to get rid of the ego. I just think there's no room for an ego when you're parenting. I have always felt that ego is a safe haven for people in pain to hide. They don't know they're doing it. It's their protection mechanism. But when you have that wall up, all you can do is feel your own stuff. And when you have children it's not about you anymore. Everything's about the child. When it becomes all about the child, if it's done in the right manner, then the wall comes down. You don't even know it.

Anita Figueredo

Physician/Co-Worker of Mother Teresa

– Mother of 9 –

I find it very easy to be friends with my children. Very easy. One thing is that you don't pull rank. Maybe your children aren't old enough yet. But when you've got them between fifty and sixty years old, you're careful not to pull rank. Their opinion is as worth listening to as yours.

All of my children are my friends. And I respect them.

Chapter 11

The Circle of Life

We don't talk enough about the whole circle. We always talk about beginnings, but we don't talk enough about the relationship of the parent and the child as they get older and how that parent-child role can change in a wonderful way.

Mary Poland

Mothers are simultaneously parents to their children and children of their parents. The women in this chapter reflect on how both these relationships evolve over time.

"How does the mother-child relationship evolve as we mature?" "What is it like to be the mother of adult children?" "How do we respond to the needs of our own aging parents?" "What complexities are involved in learning to care for the caregiver, or to accept care from our children?"

Only when we mature and face the challenges of motherhood ourselves do we really come to respect and appreciate the job our parents did when they raised us. Too often in our society aging parents are isolated and even neglected. The women in this chapter suggest that we value parents for the wise and esteemed elders they are. They see the care of elderly parents as a natural extension of their motherhood as well as an expression of their infinite gratitude. Lastly, several stress the importance of open communication between parent and child.

The circle of life entails a series of transformations. Yet, as the messages in this chapter illustrate, there are constants in all our most valued relationships—trust, love, communication, and respect.

Carmel Greenwood

Author/Entrepreneur/Lecturer

– Mother of 5 –

We teach our children, and I think too many mothers don't know how to ask for what they want. I hear a lot of "My children don't do this, they don't do that. They don't take care of me." But has anyone asked? When I ask my children, their response is immediate. They are self-absorbed, and they might not think about asking you if you need something. Sometimes it's not natural, you know. So I teach Matthew, "Oh, it's my birthday next week. I'm so excited. What are the people going to give me?"—instead of waiting around and getting nothing and pulling a long face. That's real victim behavior, and I used to do that myself. But now I remind them two weeks in advance, "What are we going to do for Mommy's birthday?" So I think it all comes down to communication. We teach people how to treat us.

Isabel Allende

Author

– Mother of 2 –

At my age most of my friends either have lost their parents or are taking care of their parents, as I do. I know that there is a point in life when the roles shift. In a way it's unavoidable, especially now that people live so long. People become ninety or one hundred years old, and somebody has to take care of them. So that's the role of the children and eventually the grandchildren.

I find it very hard to be in that position of needing care myself. I don't mind taking care of my parents at all. It's good to help them. It feels wonderful. But I would hate it if my children had to take care of me. I'm totally independent, and I don't want to be asking them for anything.

My son said some time ago, "Why would you deprive me of taking care of you, when you love doing it yourself?" I started thinking about it, but it's just that I'm so proud and so independent.

Virginia Harris

Spiritual Leader

– Mother of 3 –

The motherhood connection does change as we mature. It gets better. It gets wiser. We get gentler and more patient, and we are forgiving. I love the longer views that bring peace without complacency.

I love my motherhood maturing because it has broadened my home and hearth in service to the community and the world. I so respect our foremothers who fought so hard to get through the doors of their home into the world. The women who did get through that front door of their home made wonderful contributions. That's what I love about Mary Baker Eddy, Elizabeth Cady Stanton, Clara Barton, all of them. They got through the doors of their homes and mothered the world.

The role reversals of children caring for their parents or becoming caregivers are complex. I lived through it. I was the caregiver for an uncle who did not have any children. I think we all blossom if we have the opportunity to care. I feel that caring is inherent in each one of us. It's a quality that God ordains in us; it's natural. You often hear young children saying, "I want to help, I want to help. Let me do that, I want to help." That's what we want to do. It's something we can appreciate as we grow and develop and see that it is part of the growth and development of individuals.

As we care, it brings out feelings in us. It brings out a sense of warmth and goodness. It brings out a sense of selflessness. The Good Samaritan in the Bible—that is a very mothering, caregiving example. As we become caregivers, not just of our parents, but of the world and of others and of strangers, that act of giving balances and feeds us and checks the roughness and toughness of everyday life. I've learned through caregiving that rather than feeling put upon—"I have to go do this for my uncle or my parents, and oh, woe is me, it's a burden"—I got to see it as a blessing. It was the best dose of emotional medicine that I could have. I was better, not burdened, by helping them.

You can see why in other cultures, and in other generations, many generations lived together. I've spent a great deal of time traveling in eastern Europe before the wall came down, and I've seen some of those societies and homes. I remember one home in Russia. There were five generations living in a two-bedroom apartment. Those grandparents blessed those children. It's good emotional and spiritual medicine.

Judith Epstein

Appellate Judge

– Mother of 2 –

I don't think we necessarily experience role reversal, although for some of us who, unfortunately, are going to experience serious mental decline, we actually become infantile, and I can see where that would engender a role reversal. Generally, I would hope for an evolution of the relationship where the parents can move into becoming esteemed elders, if you will, who may have some physical frailties, but who are not in any way put into a situation where the child is the parent and the parent is the child. There are many cultures where that is exactly what happens. Many of them include taking or including the elders in the home, which I think is a wonderful model. Their opinions are sought, and their wisdom is revered.

I had the privilege of seeing my own children react to my husband's mother, who lived to be ninety-three. I think they saw a lot of that type of relationship, where she became an esteemed elder. That, to me, would be the ideal evolution of a relationship. Sometimes the medical realities prevent that, and some people just don't have the emotional predisposition for that, but that's what, idealistically, I'd like to see.

Laurel Biever

Counselor/Therapist

– Mother of 1 –

*T*he motherhood connection changes as we mature. When I think about me with my mother, it has to do with respect.

I have so much respect for what she's been through, and what she's done over time, and not just her, but any mother. As I get older and as I experience more, as I have my own daughter and see the challenges, I get more and more and more respect for her as time goes on.

As for the role reversal and caregiving for a parent or a mother, I'm sure that's extremely complex. I would hope that I continued to respect her more and more each day, and continued to remember that she knows so much more than me through her experience. I would hope I keep that in mind as she gets older and is going to need to rely on me. She will always know more than me. She continues to pave the path for what I will be doing in my life as I take from her examples of the good and the bad and try to make my life better. I hope I can keep all that in mind and not think my way is right. I can't tell you the amount of respect I have for her. I could never express it in words.

Yasmine Ahmed McGrane

Entrepreneur

– *Future mother* –

I've had a personal experience where my boyfriend's mother has gone through a lot of hardship recently and so is a lot more vulnerable, and we've tried to figure out the best advice to give her. What is the best thing we can do for her? My advice is to get back to the simple part of it. She's an amazing woman. She's raised six wonderful children along the way. And when I think of the one thing that she loves doing, it's being a mother. Even if our parents or older relatives can be more vulnerable or less strong physically or emotionally or intellectually as they get older, sometimes the number one gift we can give them is to remind them how much we need them. It may be easier to assume the role of the mother and father of your elderly parent, but sometimes what our parents most need as they get older is purpose in life. They may be retired or not taking care of children any more, and that's what they did their whole life. We can remind them that they are our parents and we still need them even if it's for little things—a little conversation on the phone where we ask their advice or ask about a story in which they grew up and what they would do in our place. Those are the things where they wake up and think, "I do have purpose. I'm still their mother."

Alexia Nye Jackson

Comedienne/Stay-at-Home Mom

– Mother of 3 –

The term "wisdom" comes to my mind right away when you find out how your respect for your mother manifests itself later. They always seem to have the wisdom as you're coming up through the years, but once you become an adult and you are in the role of mothering and your mother's maturing, you look back and realize what you couldn't possibly have known until you got there yourself. It's like being in the trenches of any engagement or battle. As a parent you are always trying to understand what the next unexpected event is and trying to plan your strategy to make sure that your love is manifest in the right way. What is the right thing? Is it a disciplinary action? Is it a big hug? Now here you are with someone who's already done all that, and you finally recognize that because you're there. You look back and you feel respect for her wisdom and her sacrifice and for all the things that you're living. I mean you absolutely have to give to that person and take care of that person. Tell her what a great mother she is and how great she was in those active years, and that you just adore her.

Calle Anderson

Artist/Sculptor

– Mother of 2 –

I'm actually dealing with the issue of how to become the caregiver as my mother and father seem a little more vulnerable. I talked to my sister about it last night, this very tender issue of how we think and how we would feel safe about them and at the same time respect them as our parents and as people who have always made their own decisions. I think part of their sense of their own independence is that they love their home, they don't have a lot of help, and they're just wonderful. Then all of a sudden some of us think my father shouldn't be driving. It's a very hard thing to love and support and be available and be very gentle about these issues around aging.

I think what we all really want from parents as they get older is direction. I find guessing what might be right, trying to figure out what the right degree of involvement is, very hard. It would be wonderful if parents were forthcoming about what they want. Things change, and their lives change. It helps a lot if we're given advice and given clues.

Communication really helps. On Sunday I had a couple over who are my parents' friends. They said that their kids had wanted them to move. They had stairs in their house, and the kids worried about that. Finally they said to the kids, "Leave us alone. We love our house. We're going to stay here." They ended up both getting knee replacement surgery and staying in their house. That's what they wanted to do. But the kids were thinking, "You can't live there, and you've got to get this, and you've got to go here and go there." You just don't know what that dynamic should be.

After I had this lunch with these friends of my parents, I called my sister and said, "You're not going to believe what they said." My sister and I pored over their remarks about how they felt and what they wanted their kids to do. So often we as the children just don't know.

The other thing that has really helped me is that I have a sister and four brothers. My sister and I talk to each other all the time and check in on these issues. So it has worked out. For instance, both my sister and I live out of town from my parents. I go to see my parents every six weeks, and my sister goes to see them every six weeks. So every three weeks one of us is visiting for a few days. They're perfectly healthy, but I think it gives them a feeling that they're very important and that we're there for them.

Gretchen DeWitt

Public Relations

– Mother of 2 –

A real tragedy in this country is that children move out of the city or out of the state. We are so transient. We don't have the same setup as Europeans do or the Chinese do or the Arabs do. We don't have that community that cares for the elderly, and so they're put into homes. I've told my children if they put me there, I'm leaving whatever I have left over to See's Candy or something. I don't want to be put someplace if I don't have dementia or Alzheimer's. Rest homes just look so abandoned.

At some point, the roles are reversed. Babies are born and they don't have hair or teeth, and they wear diapers, and that's the way we exist most of the time. We are gumming our food, we lose our hair, and we're in diapers some of the time. We become babies. Hopefully our children love us enough to help us through this period of our lives. People need to be surrounded by love all their lives, and particularly when they're feeling so vulnerable physically and mentally and emotionally. Babies die without love. They just shrivel up and die if they aren't held. I think old people do, too. They need to be touched and talked to and cared about, or they stop living.

Stacy Friedman

Rabbi

– Mother of 2 –

The more respect we give to our children, the more they will learn respect. I see it as my parents are starting to age. I need to start paying attention to them and to their needs, and just take care of them. I think if we treat our children with respect and demonstrate love by taking care of them, then that will return to us.

Sharon Cohn

Entrepreneur

– Mother of 4 –

It's hard. You see your mother getting frail and older, and it's hard for us not to see our mothers as strong. It's hard to be the ones who can take charge and take care of her in all ways. That is what she always did. But you totally understand what she sacrificed and gave to you during the time that you were a child, and as her child you wouldn't give anything less to her. You can never repay what she has done for you, but being able to support her in whatever way she needs is something that's just understood for me. No matter what, she'll always be Mom.

Amy Apollo Ahumada

Boutique Manager

– Mother of 2 –

Something that is so sad in our society, particularly because it's very different in other societies, is how the elders are not respected and appreciated and loved. They are very much dismissed and put in homes and forgotten about. They're lucky if they get a visit once a month or even once a year. If you're in a third-world country where the family works together to eat, there's so much more of a family environment. In our society, children grow up and go out on their own to make a life for themselves. I think that people get way too caught up and take their working life way too seriously. Sometimes it's such a challenge to keep a good job and be good at it and then take care of your family on top of it, so that taking on anything else, like caring for your mother, feels like a burden. But I could never imagine putting my mother in a home and not taking care of her.

Gretchen de Baubigny

Community Volunteer/Consultant

– Mother of 2 –

We set an example for our children by the way we've cared for them when they've been ill or fragile, and that is ingrained in them. I've learned, too, that I have to give my children the opportunity to take care of me, because if I don't I'm denying them the great satisfaction that I have as a mother caring for them. I think we're role models of care-giving, and they learn from us, but it's also important to let our fragile natures come out once in a while. It has to be a step-by-step, gradual thing rather than an avalanche.

Barbara Rosenberg

Community Volunteer/Philanthropist

– Mother of 2 –

It's tough, because parents are living longer. But it isn't always a matter of age. Some children have a great sense of responsibility and are the caregivers to an inadequate mother very early in their childhood. In my own family, one daughter in-law has always been a caregiver to her mother and continues to be. So I'm not sure it's always an age thing. However, as people grow older and frailer, we're seeing more the necessity of being a caregiver. It's vital that we begin to address this in familial relationships, that the roles will change. Decisions have to be made by children—financial decisions and care decisions, a whole variety of things. Parents also have to learn that at a given point in their life they perhaps have to let go. They won't be able to handle everything, and they need to plan for that while they're still able to do so. This is a whole area that previous generations didn't have to consider. People died at age sixty, and the children were immersed in raising their own families. I think sociologists and family psychologists and children themselves are going to need to look at this. Children need some training and help and conditioning to accept that responsibility.

Carol Bartz
Entrepreneur
– Mother of 1 –

There's always that pivotal point when your children do see that you are vulnerable. The first time they see you cry, the first time they see you in pain, the first time they see you out of the mother character, that's a very pivotal time that only continues pivoting as you really do need help. That help might be emotional support or physical support or maybe even financial support, and then eventually the ultimate, and that is the frailty of old age and so forth. What do they say? "You reap what you sow." If you want your kids to be there for you and with you, you should have been there for and with them.

Mary Poland
Philanthropist/Stay-at-Home Mom
– Mother of 1 –

I think that I am personally better equipped to deal with the role reversal in my own future than my parents were.

I've watched how my mother passed away from Alzheimer's and how I had to deal with my father. It absolutely has been role reversal. I have stepped in and become like an older sister to my dad. I had to have some very tough-love discussions with him about how he's living his life and how he could improve the quality of his life. I've been the caretaker for him. He ended up being the caretaker for Mom for many, many years, and it was really hard on him. It took its toll on him physically and emotionally, and I watched this happen. I can take those lessons and apply them in my own life and be more receptive to understanding that the roles will reverse for me some day and be okay with it. I can see that happening and be very aware of it.

Right now I'm still in the mothering part of it. My son is not yet into his twenties. I'm also the kind of mom who experiences greater and greater joy as my child gets older, because I can have much more mature discussions with him, and that just thrills me. The connection for me just gets to be better and more alive as he gets older. I look forward to the adult stages with him. Certainly the mothering goes away in a certain aspect, but I'll enjoy us discussing things on an equal level. I'm looking forward to him teaching me things and keeping an open mind to all sorts of ways that he can introduce subjects that maybe I won't have as much access to as I grow older.

It's the circle of life, and I celebrate in the circle of life. This comes back to the reason why we have children. It starts the circle of life up again, and there's something very natural and very rhythmic about it. The roles will change. This should be celebrated. There should probably be some discussion about that not being something that should be so fearful. Let's celebrate. Taking on a different role of being watched over by your older children is just as exciting as the new role of being a mother. It's a transition that should be celebrated just as much, because it's very natural.

We don't talk enough about the whole circle. We always talk about beginnings, but we don't talk enough about the relationship of the parent and the child as they get older and how that parent-child role can change in a wonderful way. We should always anticipate change and embrace it and celebrate in it.

Arlene Ackerman

School Superintendent

– Mother of 2 –

I never really got to care for my mother because she died so quickly. She was diagnosed with lung cancer. They told us we would have eighteen months, probably, before she would die. The last time I talked to her was on my birthday, and she actually went in the hospital the next day. I was going to go home and start spending a week at a time with her because I knew I had a year and a half. She died that Friday morning, two hours before I was to take a plane to get there. I would have done anything to care for my mother, but I never got the chance to do so. I thought it would get easier with time, but it hasn't. There is not a Mother's Day that rolls around that I don't feel this great loss. I hate to look at Mother's Day advertisements and stuff. It hurts me so.

Now my dad has had several strokes, and he's in a lung care facility. I find it a privilege to go back and take care of him. I really do. I wish I lived there so I could do it more. I don't mind feeding him. I don't mind bathing him. I don't mind changing his diaper. It's about giving back. It's about being a friend. It's about loving unconditionally, only the roles change. I guess that's the way I look at this, and I hope my sons will be able to do that for me. I think when you have unconditional love, when you are friends, you are able to do it. You are able to turn those roles around and proudly say, "It's my turn, and I gladly serve," because you know that your mom did it for you.

You know, sometimes when I get really sick or something, I still call out her name. I do. I call out "Mom." Because that's who I think of when I'm sick. I'd have given anything to be a caregiver for my mother, anything. You owe them your life. It's about love.

Donna Radu

Equity Trader/Stay-at-Home Mom

– Mother of 2 –

The older my children get, the more they grow into their life and let go of Mom. As they develop and create their own lives and families, I know the momentum will pick up and I will start to get on with things in terms of my own life. It's my opportunity to create and maintain my own life. I really want to work on taking care of myself, because I don't feel my mother has maintained her own life. Her life has always been about her kids, and it's still about her kids. She waits for us all the time. She waits for us to call and wants to see us. She kind of stopped everything when she went through the change of life. I want to continue to grow. I always want my kids to come unconditionally and feel okay about it and not have to feel like "Oh, we need to go take care of Mom." As I mature and as I grow younger, as my grandmother used to say, and as my children's lives start to unfold, I feel I have an obligation and an opportunity to create and maintain a life that both my kids and I are really proud of. They're proud of me now. I want them to be proud of me as I get older, and I want them to remember everything about me, all the qualities.

I hope I can stick with that and that I don't lose my momentum, and I hope I can let go of my kids. I want to be able to let them have their own life and walk their walk. And of course my kids will always know, as I did, that they can come home at any time and any age and under any circumstances.

As far as being the caregivers, my mother's mother was a big influence. It's almost like we had two mothers for a long time. We took care of my grandmother, my sisters and I, more so than my mother. We gave her a reason to keep living. It was so easy taking care of her, because she gave us so much love.

My sisters, my brother, and I have all taken care of my mom's mom, and we all currently share a role in taking care of our parents today. Where there's great love, there's compassion, and caregiving comes naturally. We all have our own lives and live in separate places, but it just comes naturally for us. We know it's part of our life.

Chapter 12

Motherhood Lasts Forever

Life begins with motherhood, and the spirit

of motherhood lives on in our souls and

in our hearts for generations.

DONNA RADU

*T*his chapter is the summation of the thoughts and stories that these twenty-seven incredible women shared with me for this book. Many of them closed their interviews with a favorite quotation—some from a treasured source, others in their own words—to serve as a coda to their life messages.

At the heart of the philosophies and feelings found in this chapter is the realization that motherhood lasts forever. Motherhood is the one irrevocable relationship we experience in life. It is transcendent, leaving an enduring legacy in the hearts of our children. .

Motherhood is creativity in its purest form. It is the golden thread connecting life and love, and we, as women, are blessed with the role of the perpetuators of life! As you read the words in this chapter, let the thoughts of these women elevate your spirit and renew your consciousness to the miracle that is motherhood.

Carmel Greenwood

Author/Entrepreneur/Lecturer

– Mother of 5 –

I think my favorite quote is "Never give up." Sometimes children lead you to the point of complete exasperation, but there's always that connection, no matter what.

I think motherhood never ends. Even when the children are adults having their own children, you're still mother, just to be there. Not to do it for them, but to be there, is the most important gift that you can give.

When your children are young, you think, "When they grow up, I'll be free." Actually, it's worse. You're never free. But you wouldn't want to be free. There's always that connection.

The greatest joy to me now, having five children, is Christmases and celebrations. It's a joy to see their faces and how they've grown, and to remember our different experiences together. It's such a gift of abundance to participate in that.

I consider myself extremely lucky to have had five children. They've taught me a lot, and they've pulled me up constantly. It's really been a gift, and it will never end. Nor would we want it to.

Isabel Allende

Author

– Mother of 2 –

I think that motherhood lasts forever, even after your children are dead. Yes, it does. Then it's prolonged through your grandchildren in fantastic ways. For me it has been very rewarding. It has lasted forty years, and I think it will last to the last day of my life.

My philosophy about motherhood is that you do the best you can and you shouldn't feel guilty if things don't work out, because life has ways of forcing people to do things that you think should not be done. I am a different product from what my parents wanted me to be, and so are my children. I never did anything on purpose to harm them, but I did harm them in many ways without knowing. I can't feel guilty about it. I did the best I could with the knowledge I had at that moment. And I am not the only influence in their lives. They have a father, they have the world around them, they have their own lives to lead, and there are things that happen in people's lives. It would be an act of arrogance to believe that whatever they are today is a result of what I have done with them or for them, or have not done with them or for them. I'm just one factor in their lives, and not even the main one.

Virginia Harris

Spiritual Leader

– Mother of 3 –

I think motherhood lasts forever. Those mothering qualities are natural and really divinely natural to each one of us, women or men, girls or boys, whether we birth children or not, whether we adopted them or never had them. It's what balances the expressions of our lives and keeps us whole.

I often go back to a quote from *Science and Health*, by Mary Baker Eddy, who, as I've said, is one of my great mentors. She says, "Father-Mother is the name for Deity, which indicates His tender relationship to His spiritual creation."

She was such a proponent of the motherhood of God. Her writings are just filled with it, and writing as she did in 1875 was a very courageous thing to do. I love to think of those words about the name of the Deity being Father-Mother, and how that speaks of His tender relationship to His spiritual creation.

Jennifer Morla

Entrepreneur/Designer

– Mother of 2 –

When you go through the newspaper and you see another woman in another country who is not dressed like you, perhaps is not of the same skin color, and she's holding that child in her hands, being a mother, you are that person with the child in your hands. It breaks down all cultural barriers. It is so universal. When I see that, I am feeling the pain of that mother right then, because you know what that would be. It's universal, and you are so humbled by it. Not that I didn't have that viewpoint before, but it resonates with me so strongly now. That I am a mother really magnifies the human condition. You feel it. You absolutely feel it.

Judith Epstein

Appellate Judge

– Mother of 2 –

Motherhood is truly the only irrevocable relationship, so, yes, it lasts forever. I guess legally you could sever those rights, but you would never stop being a mother. That's why I prefer my children to call me Mom, or Mother, instead of my name. I went through a phase, as so many children do, of wanting to call my mother by her first name. She said to me, quite firmly, "I am your only mother, and I would prefer it if you called me Mother, because no one else can call me that." I've always honored that, and happily so.

I did give some thought to a quote that sums up my philosophy. Actually, it's one I created, so here's my motto, which I just made up today: "Fill their souls with love, but leave room for their own desire."

Ann Getty

Philanthropist/Interior Designer

– Mother of 4 –

I think motherhood lasts forever. I will always be my children's mother. Sometimes I'll even be right.

As for a quote—I'm laughing, because there is one that I use on my granddaughter. It is not a favorite quote so much as one that I get a laugh out of. It is from the movie *Matilda*: "I'm smart; you're dumb; I'm big; you're little. And there's nothing you can do about it."

Laurel Biever

Counselor/Therapist

– Mother of 1 –

I certainly hope that motherhood lasts forever. The four years I've been a mother have been the most fulfilling, the most beautiful experience I've had in my life. I cannot imagine that this kind of feeling and love would ever diminish. And I can't imagine anything ever taking away the intensity and the connection that I feel toward my own mother. I believe it lasts forever.

Children are a gift, a blessing from God. They are just on loan to us. We're here to take care of them and guide them and then, when we have to, release them and let them grow and be on their own. And that's not when they turn eighteen. That's every day, continually releasing little bits. They're on loan to us, and we're fortunate to have them in our lives.

Yasmine Ahmed McGrane

Entrepreneur

– Future mother –

I do think motherhood lasts forever, though it goes through stages. I'm actually a lot closer now to my parents because I have a lot more compassion toward them in terms of things I didn't understand—reasons why my dad was so hard and disciplinarian, my mother's background. I didn't understand it all growing up. I wished I was like everybody else and could have parents born and raised in America and just fit in. Now I look at it and think I'm so fortunate because I've had such wonderful parents who have had so many tough and wonderful experiences in their life. They overcame so much, and yet they gave so much love to us.

When all is said and done, motherhood and fatherhood absolutely last forever. We Americans, especially, grow farther apart over time. With family members living in all different states or all different countries, it's really important to maintain that connection. When I say connection, it's not just a conversation once in a while about the day-to-day stuff in our life. It's actually understanding who your parents are, understanding what they've done in their life and letting them tell the stories to you so you learn from them and pass them on to your grandchildren. It's a wonderful process if you can open up the door and it's all at the right time. For me it's only happened more recently that I've actually wanted to hear these stories from my parents, and it's really helped me become the person I am.

To sum up, I think motherhood is the purest form of creativity one can have. If you allow it to, that creativity opens up so many other doors in your self. Your own passions that maybe have been put on the back burner can come out. Learn from your children, inspire them, inspire yourself, and you'll definitely enjoy the little things of being a mother.

Alexia Nye Jackson

Comedienne/Stay-at-Home Mom

– Mother of 3 –

A mother definitely lasts forever. It's almost like asking if your breath is there until you're gone. Motherhood lasts forever, and it should absolutely last forever.

It's so much bigger than that, too—just the image of mother, motherhood, and the Madonna as this safe haven lasts forever. But in terms of me having raised my children into adulthood and knowing that was a part of my life, yes, that lasts forever, and it leaves its mark. And it's a good thing.

The one thing I would add is that today being a mother is this private thing, too much so. There's not enough regard or enough respect for it. It should be really highly regarded, and people should know that about you. You can't shout it loud enough. If people don't know about that part of you and they inquire about that, it should be something that takes at least ten minutes to talk about—you know, to tell your kid's age or how many you have, to impart one good thought about it or something you remember. Motherhood lasts in a big and magnificent and wonderful and overwhelming way, and the sooner the world recognizes it, the better we'll all be.

I guess I would offer my own little quote: "You have to revel in the jumping on the bed moments." That's what you have got to do. Keep jumping on the bed. It's all good.

Calle Anderson

Artist/Sculptor

– Mother of 2 –

Motherhood is my connection to life. With my daughter and my son, if they're far away or if they don't live in the same town I do now, I feel completely connected to them at all times. It's my job to make sure that happens. I don't keep score—"I called him twelve times; he's called me once." I never do it. We talked twelve times. It doesn't matter who called whom.

Elizabeth Colton

Philanthropist/Women's Advocate

– Mother of 2 –

Motherhood definitely lasts forever. I haven't had any grandchildren yet, but I understand that once you get into that role, the mothering and nurturing are awakened again in a whole new way.

We're all growing together, and our roles change as we grow. We have to appreciate that and be open to it and help guide it when we can. One of my biggest challenges is not being too hard on myself about how I fulfilled that role. Think of how our generations have changed. Our parents had a totally different view of what their relationship with us should and would be, and we didn't turn out too badly. I think we have to have a little faith in our kids that, as hard as we tried, they'll turn out all right too.

Gretchen DeWitt

Public Relations

– Mother of 2 –

One quote I would choose comes from Abraham Lincoln: "All that I am, or hope to be, I owe to my angel mother."

I just love being a mother. My children both got married in the last year, and it's a fulfillment of bliss for me because I see them have what I wanted. I see them start a new part of their lives, and I look forward to seeing their children being born and loving them.

I love this cycle of life, so I will always value my role as a mother more than anything I have, and I will value my children more than anything I have and more than anyone I know, including my husband. They are the people I would run into the burning house for first. He'd have to get his own way out of the window somehow. I'd go for the children.

Tricia LaVoice

Psychologist/Stay-at-Home Mom

– Mother of 4 –

When it's all said and done, living without my children would be like living without air to breathe. I take that on for me. I have a lot of friends who have fabulous lives and who don't have children, and some who do. So I say that for my life. There could have been no other way for me to reach happiness. I have some things in my life that you could look at and think, wow, that's a tough life. Actually I feel like I'm the happiest, luckiest woman in the world because I've got my babies, and I've got a great husband. For me there could have been no other way to reach that level of peace and happiness.

The most important phrase about mothering for me is something Meryl Streep said in a movie, I think it was *Bridges of Madison County*: "The mother needs to stand still so everyone can dance around her." I so believe that. Standing still doesn't have to mean that you can't have a life outside of your children or have a career, but it does mean you have to be able to handle everything that you have chosen to take on outside of your parenting. You need to be able to stand still so they feel that there's a base there that's secure, that's solid, and that they can go to at any time.

Jeannie Brown

Entrepreneur

– Mother of 3 –

You are always a mother, under any conditions and whatever you did throughout your life. If there were disagreements along the line and you've parted, or whatever you have done, you are always a mother. As long as you live, to be a good mother is the greatest joy in the world. My favorite quote is something I said earlier: "Having children is like reliving your life again." I'm seventy-six, my daughter is fifty-five, and she reminds me of when I was fifty-five. Our children make us feel young. "What's old is new again, and that lasts forever."

Stacy Friedman

Rabbi

– Mother of 2 –

There have been times when I've spoken with women who have lost children or had miscarriages or had to have abortions, and I said to them, "You are a mother." I think that motherhood happens before the child is born, even if the child is never born. Motherhood lasts even if, God forbid, a child dies. Motherhood lasts forever because motherhood is really about that love. That's why women can adopt children. Motherhood is not only about that biological bond. It's something that is a lot deeper than that. It's really in your heart.

Nothing can ever take any of those experiences away. So motherhood lasts forever, and I think the love and the pain that go with it last forever and probably get deeper and deeper over time.

Benita Potters

Entrepreneur/Community Volunteer

– Mother of 2 –

Motherhood does last forever, no question. Do I have a favorite quote? Yes, it's that proverb about roots and wings: "The most important thing we can give our children is roots and wings."

Sharon Cohn

Entrepreneur

– Mother of 4 –

I totally agree that motherhood lasts forever. It just changes. There are different times and phases that it goes through. But you're always the mom, no matter what. You'll always have the worries, and you'll always have the love, and you'll always have the frustrations. All that will always be there, just in a different way.

The bottom line is for your children to be happy. That's why you care. That's why you go through the ups and downs. You don't want them to have to go through some of the processes that they have to go through to find their happiness. But it's going to last forever no matter what, and that feels really good. That feels wonderful.

When I was born, my dad's quote was "I am undone with joy." Every day my mom lived that joy. I think if we remember that joy of our child being born into our lives every day when we wake up, and if we go through the thankfulness for the opportunity of having motherhood in our lives, it will be so much easier to get through the day. "I am undone with joy" is something that always stuck with me and always made me feel wanted. It just makes me so thankful for my mom and my dad and that I was chosen to be in their lives, and thankful that my children were chosen to be in my life.

Sylvia Boorstein
Author/Buddhist Teacher

– Mother of 4 –

The quote that comes to mind about motherhood is in the beginning of *The Story of Ferdinand*. You remember that Ferdinand the bull is different from all the other bulls. Unlike the other bulls that run around and snort and fight with each other, Ferdinand likes to sit under his favorite cork tree and smell the flowers. Ferdinand's mother worries about him being different from the other bulls, and she worries that he will be lonesome. But there is a line that says that because she is an understanding mother, she lets him sit by himself under the cork tree and smell the flowers and be happy. I love that, because it's a statement about mothers and their relationship with children.

Amy Apollo Ahumada
Boutique Manager
– Mother of 2 –

You continue to be a mother forever. I can't wait to be a grandmother and a great-grandmother. The operative word is "mother."

My main quote that encompasses it for me is from the book *Love You Forever* by Robert Munsch, and it goes, "I'll love you forever / I'll like you for always / As long as I'm living / My baby you'll be."

Gretchen de Baubigny
Community Volunteer/Consultant
– Mother of 2 –

Oh my gosh, does it last forever. If they had told that to me when I was bearing children, I would have denied it and said, "Oh, no, they turn twenty-one and they're out. I'm done." Well, do you know why it lasts forever? Because I wouldn't have it any other way.

I love Kahlil Gibran and I like his poem about your children: "Your children are not your children. / They are the sons and daughters of Life's longing for itself. / They come through you but not from you / And though they are with you, yet they belong not to you." And this is what I hang on to: "You are the bows from which your children as living arrows are sent forth. / The archer sees the mark upon the path of the infinite, and He bends you with His might that His arrows may go swift and far."

Whether it's a joyful thing, or whether it's painful to watch them move to New York or get on the Concorde and be back and forth to Paris every week, I think of those words. Let the bow be strong, because that arrow's going to go swift and far. I believe we all have our own journeys. I can't put any fences around my children, nor do I want to. They will go swift and far, and they will celebrate it because they're doing it their way. But they know that I will never abandon them.

Barbara Rosenberg

Community Volunteer/Philanthropist

– Mother of 2 –

I guess you're always a mother, particularly to your children. I think it's a state of mind, a state of being, and a state of doing. I recently received a phone call from the sister of somebody who I taught in high school. This young woman, Patty, has been stricken with cancer. Her sister had to go back to Denver, and she asked if I would make sure during the week to stop in at the hospital to see Patty. Patty's mother's gone. To some extent that's the role of a mother, I think, to be a friend and to be comforting. Giving a nurturing aspect and a sense of making people feel comfortable and cared about is the role of motherhood, and I don't think it's limited to your own children or to your own family. Nor do I think it's limited to women. It's limited to any aspect of humanity that calls upon you to give whatever gifts you can share.

Carol Bartz

Entrepreneur

– Mother of 1 –

Motherhood lasts forever, but I think you have to be very careful that you don't become a burden to your children. Somehow we believe we have the right to control our children forever. We do not have that right. We don't own them. I think we have to be very careful of that.

When you look at most of nature, parents let go of their offspring very quickly, and it's over. They don't hang around together. They're gone. The cubs don't hang with the lioness. They have to go find another territory. We are blessed that we get to stay connected, but we can't abuse that. We have to enjoy our kids every minute of the day and just feel blessed that we are allowed to have them. I think it's as simple as that.

Mary Poland

Philanthropist/Stay-at-Home Mom

– Mother of 1 –

Motherhood lasts forever, but you keep it in perspective with your life. It doesn't define you. It enhances you.

It is what brings out the best in people, too. From where I come from, having to work so hard to get Stratton, he was such a gift that that's why every day is something exciting. I feel like somebody handed him to me. I don't own my child. He's not my property, not my possession. He is something that somebody's asked me to nurture, to take care of, to love, and to springboard.

I can just see a mother bird saying, "Now you get to fly," and the joy is to see them fly. There isn't anything better than that.

Arlene Ackerman

School Superintendent

– Mother of 2 –

Even when you are no longer here on this earth, you're in the hearts of your children, and hopefully their children. You leave a legacy, and you pass on the richness of your history and who you were as a person, and it lives in those who follow. Every day I'm thankful for an opportunity to call Anthony and Matthew my sons. Motherhood is a gift from God.

Donna Radu

Equity Trader/Stay-at-Home Mom

– Mother of 2 –

When it's all said and done, motherhood never dies. Everything I do today is going to go on for generations and generations. Life begins with motherhood, and the spirit of motherhood lives on in our souls and in our hearts for generations. I feel that everything in life is mortal except for a mother's love. I think motherhood equals immortality. At times I still feel my grandmother in the same room. She's been gone for almost seven years now, and I still get the urge to call her and fill her in on what's going on. A lot of times things happen and I think, "I can't wait to call Nana." And she's been gone for a long time. But she's still in all of us.

I do have a quote. I found it in a book called *Mother's*

Nature, by Andrea Alban Gosline, that I bought years ago. I just opened it today and found this. It says, "To anticipate the joy and love of tomorrow, to flourish as a woman and mother, to nurture yourself as you nurture your loved ones, to wonder at the natural world, to voice your thoughts more clearly, to stand for your children, to listen more thoughtfully, to envision a happier, more peaceful life, to embrace your circle of friends and family and find that you've always belonged. We wish you safe passage on your journey into motherhood."

Ariel Bybee

Mezzo-Soprano/Voice Teacher

– Mother of 1 –

My religious belief is that life is eternal and that life goes on, and I believe that in the next life we will be with all our families. That's a great hope that I have. These relationships that we have are the most important thing we carry with us into the next life, and it's important to invest time in relationships that are eternal.

I don't know what we'll be like then, but I think we'll all be friends. I think we'll all love one another. We'll be equals in our relationships, and we'll go on and on. So the investments that we put into those relationships now will pay off in the next life.

Anita Figueredo

Physician/Co-Worker of Mother Teresa

– Mother of 9 –

Being a mother is absolutely marvelous. I wouldn't trade

a minute of it. I wouldn't trade any part of it, not even the sorrow of the children I lost.

That reminds me of another story about Mother Teresa. I had lost my eighteen-month-old son. He was our youngest child. The first time he learned how to open these two doors that opened onto the lily pond, he went out and tripped and fell into the pond and drowned.

I wrote Mother and told her that he had died. I was just keeping her up on the family because she was always very interested. And she wrote the most remarkable condolence that I have ever received, or ever heard of.

She wrote back and said that she was so glad that Bobby had died because she had just founded a group of nine young men who were to be Brothers, and she was looking for a patron for them. She wanted to find somebody who was very close to God but who had nothing else to do. So none of the major saints qualified at all. She said she would take Bobby and make him their patron, and he still is. She gave him the responsibility of caring for the Brothers, and they're doing great. You know, if he'd lived to be a hundred, he wouldn't have accomplished that.

She was the definition of motherhood. I have the final letter that she wrote on the day she died, September 5, 1997. She wrote it in her own hand, and then it was taken away to be typed. It was brought back for her signature, but she died before she was able to sign it. Shall I read it to you?

"My Dearest Children,

"This brings you Mother's love, prayer and blessing that each one of you may be only all for Jesus through Mary. I know that Mother says often 'Be only all for Jesus through Mary,' but that is because that is all Mother wants for you, all Mother asks from you. If in your heart you are only all for Jesus through Mary, and if you do everything only all for Jesus through Mary, you will be a true MC." An MC is a Missionary of Charity. The letter continues, "Thank you for all the loving wishes you sent for Society Feast. We have much to thank God for, especially that he has given us Our Lady's spirit to be the spirit of our society. Loving trust and total surrender made Our Lady say yes to the message of the angel, and cheerfulness made her run in haste to serve her cousin Elizabeth. That is so much our life. Say yes to Jesus and running in haste to serve him in the poorest of the poor. Let us keep very close to Our Lady, and she will make that same spirit grow in each one of us."

She writes a bit more about Mary and about having a spirit of thankfulness. Then she concludes with some thoughts about Saint Therese of Lisieux, who is called the Little Flower. She was a young and very saintly Carmelite nun, very devoted to Jesus, who died of tuberculosis at the age of 24. The pope had just decided to honor her with the exalted title of Doctor of the Church.

Mother writes, "And now I've heard that Jesus is giving us one more gift. This year, one hundred years after she went home to Jesus, Holy Father is declaring Little Flower to be a Doctor of the Church. Can you imagine, for doing little things with great love the Church is making her a Doctor, like Saint Augustine and the big Saint Theresa? It's just like Jesus said in the Gospel to the one who was seated in the lowest place, 'Friend, come up higher.' So let us keep very small and follow Little Flower's way of trust and love and joy, and we will ful-fill Mother's promise to give saints to Mother Church."

That's the end of the letter. She wrote that, and then she died. Imagine having that be your final thought.

Contributors

Dr. Arlene Ackerman has served in public education for thirty-four years and is currently Superintendent of the San Francisco Unified School District. She received her doctorate in Administration, Planning and Social Policy through the Harvard Graduation School of Education, Urban Superintendents Program. She also holds a master's degree in education from Harvard University and in educational administration and policy from Washington University, St. Louis. Dr. Ackerman has received numerous honors and awards, including appointments to the President's Board of Advisors on Historically Black Colleges and Universities, the College Boards' Commission on Writing in America's School and Colleges, and the Teaching Commission. She is the mother of two sons.

Amy Apollo Ahumada graduated from American Conservatory Theatre in San Francisco, California. She is a filmmaker, poet, nature lover, and the manager of What Women Want, a boutique in San Rafael, California. She writes, however, that her greatest accomplishment by far was giving birth to her two boys, River and Koa. "In my dream life I would be hanging out with my kids, doing art, laughing, playing, building, cooking, tickling, reading, and making mud pies. My children complete me and allow me to live each day to the fullest, to love beyond the boundaries of love itself. It is love beyond description and the best feeling in the world. I thank them for making the sun shine every day of my life."

ISABEL ALLENDE is an internationally acclaimed author. She is the mother of two children and a grandmother. Born in Peru, she was raised in Chile. She went into exile after her uncle, Chilean president Salvador Allende, was overthrown and killed in a CIA-assisted coup in 1973. A journalist for many years, she began writing fiction in 1981. All of her works have a common theme: life is precious and should be free from oppression. Her novels feature female protagonists whose strength, intelligence, and creativity enable them to endure hardships, fight oppression, and improve the world around them. Her books have been translated into twenty-seven languages, and two of them were made into movies and theatre plays. Her published works include *Aphrodite: A Memoir of the Senses*; *Of Love and Shadows*; *Eva Luna*; *The Stories of Eva Luna*; *Infinite Plan*; *Paula*; *Daughter of Fortune*; *Portrait in Sepia*; *City of the Beasts*; *My Invented Country*; *Kingdom of the Golden Dragon*; and the international best-seller *The House of the Spirits*.

CALLE ANDERSON is an artist and sculptor who demonstrates solo and group art exhibitions all over the world. She received her master's degree in fine arts at the San Francisco Art Institute, San Francisco. She has also studied at Studio School, New York; Art Student's League, New York; Manhattanville College; Otis Art Institute, Los Angeles; and the University of California, Los Angeles. She is the mother of two children.

CAROL BARTZ is the mother of one daughter. She is Chairman of the Board, President and CEO of Autodesk, Inc., the world's leading supplier of design software. Appointed to President Bush's Council of Advisors on Science and Technology, she is one of a select group of industry leaders expected to play a key role in shaping the federal government's high-tech agenda. She holds an honors degree in computer science from the University of Wisconsin and is the recipient of numerous awards and honors, including an honorary Doctor of Human letters degree from the New Jersey Institute of Technology, an honorary Doctor of Science degree from Worchester Polytechnic Institute, and an honorary Doctor of Letters degree from William Woods University.

LAUREL BIEVER is a licensed professional counselor and a loving mother, daughter, sister, and friend. She has spent three and a half years focusing on raising her daughter, grieving the loss of her husband, and being actively involved in her church. Currently a part-time therapist at the Gestalt Associates in Columbus, Ohio, she has been involved in psychotherapy training at the Gestalt Institute of Central Ohio for many years. She earned her Masters in Education at the University of Dayton, in Dayton, Ohio, and attended George Mason University in Virginia, where she met her husband and received a B.A. in psychology. She has also worked in the mental health field with a focus on incarcerated youth, chronic pain patients, and research at the Ohio State University Hospital. She has been involved in geriatric research at Johns Hopkins Hospital, and psychiatric inpatient research at Fairfax Hospital, in Virginia. She is the co-author of three published research articles relating to her research, mentioned above.

SYLVIA BOORSTEIN is a co-founding teacher of Spirit Rock Meditation Center in Woodacre, California, where she teaches mindfulness and loving kindness meditation retreats. Sylvia is the mother of four children. She earned a doctorate in psychology in 1974. She is the author of four books on mindfulness and Buddhism: *It's Easier Than You Think: The Buddhist Way to Happiness*; *Don't Just Sit There, Do Something—A Mindfulness Meditation Retreat*; *That's Funny,*

You Don't Look Buddhist: On Being a Faithful Jew and a Passionate Buddhist; and *Pay Attention, for Goodness' Sake: Practicing the Perfections of the Heart.*

JEANNIE BROWN fulfilled a lifelong dream by opening a unique coffee shop, Jeannie's Java, in Tiburon, California, after her three daughters had grown up. At the age of seventy-two, she is thrilled to see how her shop has become an award-winning success and a local treasure that people call their "home away from home." She was inspired to lead a life of service to others by the example of her mother, who worked for the Salvation Army and received many honors and awards for her dedication. Today she feels great joy in making other people happy while they visit her shop. She is the mother of three daughters and a grandmother.

ARIEL BYBEE is an Artist-in-Residence at the University of Nebraska School of Music. A mezzo-soprano, she has sung at the Metropolitan Opera for eighteen consecutive seasons. Among her leading roles at the Met are Hansel in *Hansel and Gretel*, Nichlausse in *Les Contes d' Hoffmann*, and Suzuki in *Madame Butterfly*. Before beginning her professional singing career with the San Francisco Opera Company, she taught junior high school music for five years. Since she believes that teaching refines her own performance skills, she has continued to give master classes and voice lessons on the university level. She has taught many talented singers in her New York studio, at the Lee Strasbourg Institute, and at the American Musical and Dramatic Academy. She is the mother of one daughter and a grandmother.

SHARON COHN and her husband, Bruce, have worked together on two family businesses, the B. R. Cohn Winery and the B. R. Cohn Olive Oil Company. Today Sharon is responsible for overseeing the production and marketing of

B. R. Cohn olive oils and vinegars. Before marrying Bruce, Sharon served in the United States Air Force and later worked as a dental hygienist. They live in Sonoma, California, and have raised four children.

ELIZABETH COLTON is a founding President and Board Chair of the International Museum of Women. A San Francisco resident since 1970, she is an advocate for, and philanthropist to, women's causes and San Francisco political campaigns. She also serves on the Board of Directors of Lykes Bros. Inc., a Florida-based agricultural industry corporation. A campaign consultant for more than twenty years, she directed her own political and public affairs consulting firm. Her most recent awards include Flyaway Production's "10 Women Campaign," a celebration of the risk, empowerment, and social potency of women; and the Soroptimist International of San Francisco's "Women Helping Women" award in recognition of her effective advancement of the status of women. She earned her bachelor's degree in sociology at Florida State University. She is the devoted parent of two children.

GRETCHEN DE BAUBIGNY is a philanthropist and a community volunteer in the area of education. She has also worked as a teacher and consultant of communication skills, training executives in speech skills for organization and delivery, conducting meetings, leading panel discussions, and interviews for press, radio, and television. She also conducts speech skills seminars for a number of organizations in the San Francisco Bay Area. She has taught communication skills at San Francisco Community College as well as English, speech, and drama in the Los Angeles public school system. She is the mother of two children.

GRETCHEN DEWITT has had a public relations business for over twenty years and has also been greatly involved in charity work. She grew up on a farm in Southern California, surrounded by animals and cousins. She attended La Chatelaine in Gstaad, Switzerland, and graduated from Brigham Young University with an English major and minors in Spanish and French. Her junior year was spent at Mexico City College. She has had the good fortune to have traveled extensively to far away, exotic places. She is still surrounded by animals, a loving family, and friends. She is the mother of two children

JUDITH R. EPSTEIN began her distinguished career in law in 1977. Today she is an appellate judge for the California State Bar Court. She is also an adjunct professor at the University of San Francisco School of Law, where she teaches a course in Legal Ethics. She holds a bachelor's degree in political science from the University of California, Berkeley, a master's degree in government from the University of San Francisco, and a J.D., with honors, from the University of San Francisco School of Law, where she was a member of the Law Review. She is the mother of two children.

DR. ANITA FIGUEREDO retired from medical practice in 1996, after forty-eight years of service. A native of Costa Rica, she received her medical degree in 1940 from the Long Island College of Medicine and served for many years as a doctor in San Diego County. She was the first woman to receive major surgical privileges in San Diego County. A long-time friend of Mother Teresa, she began serving as a Regional Link of the Co-Workers of Mother Teresa in 1973. Dr. Figuredo has been awarded many honors, including the Papal medal Pro Ecclesia et Pontiface; the Regional Brotherhood Award from the National Conference of Christians and Jews; and the Spirit of Unity Award from the San Diego Ecumenical Conference. She is a lady of the Order of the Holy Sepulcher of Jerusalem, having been awarded the highest rank, the Grand Cross. She is the founder of the Friends of the Poor, Inc., a charity support-ing services to the destitute in Mexico and Africa. Dr. Figuredo also serves as lector and Eucharistic Minister at Mary, Star of the Sea parish in La Jolla, California. Anita is the mother of nine children.

STACY FRIEDMAN is the senior Rabbi of Congregation Rodef Shalom in San Rafael, California. She has served on a vari-ety of community boards, including the board of the Marin Interfaith Youth Outreach, Marin County Interfaith Council, the Pacific Association of Reform Rabbis, and the Northern California Board of Rabbis, where she is currently vice pres-ident. She received her education at the Hebrew Union College, Jewish Institute of Religion, where she was honored with the Rabbi Jill Kreitman History Award, the Dov Bin-Num Memorial Award for Outstanding Achievement in Hebrew Language and Literature, and the Rabbi Wolli and Sarah Kaelter Scholarship Award. She graduated cum laude from Brandeis University, and also attended the Hebrew University of Jerusalem, Israel. She is the mother of two sons.

ANN GETTY is the founder and President of Ann Getty and Associates, a San Francisco-based residential interior design firm providing luxury design services and custom furniture and accessories. A designer fluent in various styles and peri-ods, she is known for sourcing her vast array of objects and opulent materials from across the globe. Additionally, her strong interest in anthropology and archeology has led her to engage in the development and recognition of craftsmen as well as the preservation of their skills. In addition to oversee-ing her world-renowned art collection, she is active in numer-ous philanthropic endeavors and opens her homes to many charitable events each year. She is also an active member of the art advisory board at Sotheby's. She is the mother of four boys and a grandmother.

CARMEL GREENWOOD was born and educated in Australia, went to Hong Kong for a two-week vacation and stayed. From humble beginnings she created her own financial investment company. She is the founder of Carmel Concepts, a company that produces tapes and other items with a spiritual message. Carmel speaks regularly at schools and to young professional organizations, as well as giving workshops around the world. She is the author of *Letting Go and Loving Life*; *Soul Energy*; and *Wake up Mum: Drugs Are Stealing Our Children*. She is the proud mother of five children, and a grandmother.

VIRGINIA HARRIS has been a staunch advocate of women and leadership, children and youth, and spirituality and health for over thirty years. She is Chairman of the Board of Trustees of The Mary Baker Eddy Library for the Betterment of Humanity and publisher of The Writings of Mary Baker Eddy. She is also Chairman of the Christian Science Board of Directors, whose religious and humanitarian activities include publishing the Pulitzer Prize-winning newspaper, *The Christian Science Monitor*. She is the mother of three sons.

ALEXIA NYE JACKSON is a writer, comedienne, visual artist, and passionate mother. Her "message of motherhood," which is to attribute economic value and social recognition to the work of mothers, has several expressions. She is currently preparing an exhibit entitled "Mother: The Job-Building Human Capital," which asserts the direct connection between the human capabilities a mother instills in her child and that child's productivity as an adult in the workforce and society thereafter. An appreciation of the more playful moments in mothering is apparent in her comedic piece "The Laundry Monologues." She is the mother of three children.

TRICIA LAVOICE is a full-time mother and wife who cares for six children—four of them her own, and a nephew and niece. Tricia and her family reside in Santa Monica, California. She holds a bachelor's degree in applied psychology from California State University, Long Beach, and a master's degree in educational psychology from Fordham University. She began a Doctoral Program in Clinical Psychology at California School of Professional Psychology but left the program after becoming pregnant with her fourth child.

YASMINE AHMED MCGRANE left a successful career in business and technology to start Maison Reve, a dream home and garden store. Born and raised in Montreal by a Swiss mother and Pakistani father, she earned her bachelor's degree in business from the University of North Carolina, Chapel Hill. She also serves as Marketing Chairperson on the board of the World Wildlife Fund, Young Partners in Conservation.

JENNIFER MORLA is President and Creative Director of Morla Design, San Francisco. With over 500 awards for excellence in graphic design, her work has been recognized by numerous organizations in the field of visual communications and is represented in the Museum of Modern Art and the Library of Congress. She has exhibitions worldwide, receiving numerous awards for her work. She is also an adjunct professor at California College of Arts and Crafts, where she teaches senior-level thesis. Jennifer is the mother of two daughters.

MARY POLAND is a philanthropist and community fundraiser. She is member of Heritage club for Kappa Kappa Gamma and the Junior League of San Francisco. She serves on the boards of the Film Institute of Northern California, the San Francisco Opera Guild and its Executive Committee, and the Ross Property Homeowners Association. She is the mother of one son.

BENTIA POTTERS is a member of the Agua Caliente Band of Cahuilla Indians. She lives in New York, and grew up in Southern California. She is on the board of two charitable organizations, the City Gardens Club of New York and the advisory board of the Association on American Indian Affairs. She manages property interests in California and is able to work mostly from home. She is the mother of two daughters.

DONNA RADU was born and raised in San Francisco and attended Catholic schools. She worked in the securities industry for eighteen years and was an institutional sales equity trader for fourteen years. She is a fulfilled wife, and now a full-time mother of two boys.

BARBARA C. ROSENBERG is a community volunteer, a grant writer for non-profit organizations, and an English teacher. She received a bachelor's degree from Brandeis University, a master's degree from Harvard University, and a doctorate degree from the University of San Francisco. She has been honored with the Scopus Award from the Hebrew University, and the Alexis de Tocqueville Award of San Francisco. She has been married for forty-eight years, and is the mother of two grown sons, and grandmother of five grandsons.